Ecstatic Soul Retrieval

draw from the richness of archetype in the collective unconscious, Brink's clients discover ways to create better, more resourceful life stories, replacing old, tired, impoverished ones. Thank you, Nick, for this valuable guide to an integrative and inclusive approach to hypnosis and ancient shamanic practices!"

PETER L. BLUM, CERTIFIED INSTRUCTOR FOR THE
NATIONAL GUILD OF HYPNOTISTS AND FACULTY MEMBER OF
DR. LEWIS MEHL-MADRONA'S COYOTE INSTITUTE

"*Ecstatic Soul Retrieval* will be invaluable for all students of the ecstatic trance postures who are interested in the psychological impact of the method. The case studies in Nick's book provide us with a wide array of material to help us understand how to use the trance postures in the field of therapy. This book will be of great help in teaching more people about the healing power of the ecstatic trance postures."

ANNETTE KI SALMEN, M.A., TEACHER AND TRAINER
OF THE CUYAMUNGUE METHOD

Ecstatic Soul Retrieval

Shamanism *and* Psychotherapy

Nicholas E. Brink, Ph.D.

Bear & Company
Rochester, Vermont • Toronto, Canada

Bear & Company
One Park Street
Rochester, Vermont 05767
www.BearandCompanyBooks.com

Bear & Company is a division of Inner Traditions International

Library of Congress Cataloging-in-Publication Data

Names: Brink, Nicholas E., 1939– author.
Title: Ecstatic soul retrieval : shamanism and psychotherapy / Nicholas E. Brink ; foreword by Stanley Krippner.
Description: Rochester, Vermont : Bear & Company , [2017] | Includes bibliographical references and index.
Identifiers: LCCN 2016041087 (print) | LCCN 2016042357 (e-book) | ISBN 9781591432616 (paperback) | ISBN 9781591432623 (e-book)
Subjects: LCSH: Ecstasy. | Trance. | Shamanism. | Mind and body. | BISAC: BODY, MIND & SPIRIT / Spirituality / Shamanism. | PSYCHOLOGY / Movements /
    Transpersonal. | SELF-HELP / Spiritual.
Classification: LCC BL626 .B74 2017 (print) | LCC BL626 (e-book) | DDC 128/.2—dc23
LC record available at https://lccn.loc.gov/2016041087

Printed and bound in the United States by Versa Press, Inc.

10 9 8 7 6 5 4 3 2 1

Text design by Priscilla Baker and layout by Debbie Glogover
This book was typeset in Garamond Premier Pro with Caxton Std, Gill Sans MT Pro, Helvetica Neue LT Std and Shelley Script LT Std as display typefaces
Artwork by M. J. Ruhe

To send correspondence to the author of this book, mail a first-class letter to the author c/o Inner Traditions • Bear & Company, One Park Street, Rochester, VT 05767, and we will forward the communication, or contact the author directly at **www.imaginalmind.net.**

Contents

Foreword

Stanley Krippner, Ph.D.

Obsessive thinking and compulsive behavior are two of the most difficult problems that clients bring to their psychotherapists. Obsessive
thoughts—for example, "Everyone I meet must like me" or "I must be
on my guard all of the time"—and compulsive behavior like drug or
alcohol addiction, sexual promiscuity, or road rage affect a number of
people and are the source of considerable suffering in this world. Most
psychologists and psychotherapists attempt to replace the repetitive,
dysfunctional self-talk heard in the narratives their clients with these
disorders tell them with positive, life-affirming thoughts or counternarratives. My old friend Milton Erickson, a renowned psychiatrist,
referred to these changes as *shifts,* reorganizations of a person's inner and
outer lives. Erickson used mental imagery, hypnosis, and dream work
with his clients to effect shifts—the same resources as those described
by Nicholas Brink in this provocative book, *Ecstatic Soul Retrieval.*
However, Brink adds another component, ecstatic trance—trance
induced with the beating of a drum as used by tribal shamans—to this
list of effective resources. He draws from the research of anthropologist
Felicitas Goodman, who discovered the power of body postures in the
trance experience, postures she believed were used by the tribal shamans
of different cultures throughout time. Though the use of shamanic
body postures and drumming may seem quite unusual and unexpected

in psychotherapy, Brink offers an effective and meaningful transition for bringing these tools to the therapeutic setting.

For millennia, the experiences of ecstatic trance, dreams, storytelling, and hypnotic-like techniques have been used by shamans to reduce suffering, deal with pain, and alleviate community discord. Over the years I have observed dozens of shamans from all six inhabited continents and have noticed that their indigenous healing methods employ all of these resources—their clients' dream reports, their clients' imagination, and their clients' ability to respond to suggestion.

For two decades I worked with Rolling Thunder, an intertribal medicine man who resided in Nevada. On one of my visits to his home he was listening to a young man's narrative of a repetitive dream, a scenario in which a white buffalo was locked in mortal combat with a black buffalo. I expected Rolling Thunder to connect the dream with a Native American prophecy concerning the birth of a white buffalo, and this approach might have been appropriate if his client, Leonard, had been Native American instead of Euro-American. Instead, Rolling Thunder listened carefully as Leonard related the dream and described the anxiety he felt upon awakening. Then the medicine man asked Leonard to close his eyes and imagine that he was observing the two fighting animals. At this point he asked, "What part of yourself do you associate with the white buffalo and what part with the black buffalo?" Leonard remained silent for a few minutes and then replied, "The white buffalo is that part of me that wants to do important work in the world, that wants to honor and heal Mother Earth, and that wants to improve the living conditions for the needy people on the planet. The black buffalo is more practical and rather selfish. It is that part of me that wants to get a good job so that I can get married, buy a house, and raise a family. During my waking hours, I am torn between those two goals, and now I understand that I am bothered by this conflict even while I am asleep." Rolling Thunder's counternarrative continued as he asked Leonard to look around at the pasture where the two buffalo were fighting. Leonard responded that the pasture went on as far as the eye could see. Rolling Thunder asked, "Don't you think there is enough room in the pasture for both buffalos? I have been working as a brakeman for the railroad for many years, and that is how I have supported my family. But that did not stop me from learning about Native American medicine and using it to help people who came my way. Soon I will start receiving a pension from the railroad and then I can devote even more of my time to following the Red Road of service." When Leonard opened his eyes, he looked as if he had attained a type of inner peace. Apparently, he had experienced what Erickson would call a "shift" and realized that his two goals were both worthy and not incompatible with each other.

There is a trickster element in shamanism, and Milton Erickson was well known for his mischievous streak. Both Erickson and tribal shamans would use certain "teaching tales" to trick their clients into getting well. Erickson often would treat compulsive behavior by encouraging his clients to indulge in even more of their dysfunctional behavior and not use their willpower to lessen the activity. Typically, the clients would stop behaving compulsively of their own accord. One night I helped Rolling Thunder treat Robert, a Native American man who had been battling alcoholism for several years. After I used hypnosis and guided imagery to enable Robert to find healthier alternatives to drinking, Rolling Thunder turned to some onlookers and offered his healing story: "I hope you all heard that owl hooting during the hypnosis session. An owl is a symbol of death, and Robert is locked in a life-and-death struggle with booze. But the owl hooted seven times, and seven is a lucky number. So I think Robert will make it." Frankly I had not heard an owl hoot at all, much less seven times, but the onlookers nodded their heads in agreement, and Robert concurred. After I left Nevada, Robert stayed on for several months, engaging in various purification rituals, working one-on-one with Rolling Thunder and receiving support from the community. After he left for home he kept in touch with Rolling Thunder for a number of years, affirming that he had maintained his sobriety.

A person's trickster is the internal mischievous manipulator/healer (like Erickson and Rolling Thunder). This inner trickster reveals to people their black buffalo, the shadow part of the self that they try to ignore. This shadow side is not necessarily negative, and when ignored it can ruin someone's life. However, when the shadow is given attention and nurtured, it can find its place in the pasture of a client's psyche, gamboling with the white buffalo and with what shamans would call "inner power animals" or personal resources, thus laying its destructive power to rest.

In this book Brink describes three of his former clients in fascinating detail—how through ecstatic trance each of them confronted and learned from their shadow side and defeated their dysfunctional parts to retrieve the parts that are healthy. Brink is a master storyteller whose teaching tales will enrich his readers' appreciation of the complexities of the human psyche. He shows how ecstatic trance, in the hands of a competent psychotherapist, can help people replace dysfunctional personal narratives with the kind of self-talk, inner stories, and positive myths that reduce if not eliminate compulsions and obsessions. The result is a life filled with purpose, direction, and joy.

Stanley Krippner, Ph.D., is professor of psychology at Saybrook University in Oakland, California, and coauthor of *The Mythic Path: A Twelve-Week Course in Personal Mythology, The Voice of Rolling Thunder: A Medicine Man's Wisdom for Walking the Red Road,* and coeditor of *The Shamanic Powers of Rolling Thunder, Healing States: A Journey into the World of Spiritual Healing and Shamanism,* and *Healing Tales: The Narrative Arts in Spiritual Traditions.*

Acknowledgments

I would like to acknowledge the Cuyamungue Institute, which promotes the original research and findings of Felicitas Goodman, who founded the institute in 1978. Dr. Goodman's work, known today as the Cuyamungue Method, focuses on the use of ancient sacred practices and postures that, when properly used, provide an experience that creates a doorway to an ecstatic experience of expanded reality. Dr. Goodman captured the essence of her work and findings in the book *Where the Spirits Ride the Wind*. I received formal training in the history and proper use of the Cuyamungue Method at the Cuyamungue Institute in Santa Fe, New Mexico. To learn more about Dr. Goodman's original work in ecstatic trance and her development and use of the Cuyamungue Method, visit the Cuyamungue Institute's website, www.cuyamungueinstitute.com.

Also I greatly appreciate the work of Meghan MacLean and the editorial staff of Bear & Co., who have given me considerable direction and assistance in organizing and editing this book.

1

Introduction to Ecstatic Trance in the Therapeutic Setting

Coyote as clown reminds us to laugh at ourselves and our problems. Laughter can come only when we gain perspective—a worry that isn't funny to us in the moment may be in a few years, once we are out from under its shadow.

LEWIS MEHL-MADRONA

I have discovered that ecstatic trance, as used by the healers and shamans of ancient and contemporary hunter-gatherer cultures, can be a very effective tool in the process of psychotherapy. I have also used hypnotic trance, another form of trance, for over forty years and have found that it too is a powerful avenue for bringing about a healthy change in the way a person experiences the world—change that helps the person overcome behavioral and emotional problems and other kinds of concerns that bring one to therapy.

Hypnotic trance and ecstatic trance are similar yet different, and some features of ecstatic trance offer an advantage over hypnotic trance. While hypnosis depends on verbal suggestions, ecstatic trance does not require such an extensive use of spoken words. Instead,

1

direction is offered by the specific body postures and what these postures express. Even more significantly, the induction ritual as developed by Felicitas Goodman leads to a higher level of spiritual maturity. Traditional psychotherapy is satisfied with the resolution of the specific psychological problems a person brings to therapy; with this resolution, the person moves beyond being absorbed in the problem that limits his or her functioning as part of their community to become a good member-in-standing of their small, defined community of like-minded people. But with the inclusion of ecstatic trance in therapy, the person further discovers the broader horizon of different cultures beyond her or his small, defined community, as well as the interdependency of all life on Earth. In this way the door is opened to becoming a citizen of the world and a steward of the Earth.

This chapter describes the nature of ecstatic trance in a therapeutic setting, and the next chapter delves into the nature and goals of psychotherapy, and specifically analytic hypnotherapy, which has many similarities to ecstatic trance for the retrieval of one's soul. Here we will see how ecstatic trance can be adapted and used as a tool in psychotherapy. Chapters 3, 4, and 5 are case studies that illustrate how this process works.

THE TOOLS OF PSYCHOTHERAPY

People who are experiencing emotional or behavioral problems often seek help from a psychologist. I began a clinical practice of psychotherapy in 1974, first for eight years in a state-run psychiatric hospital and then in private practice. There are many different methods and models for psychotherapy; mine has used dream work, hypnosis, and guided imagery as tools for accessing the unconscious mind to eventually provide relief from emotional or behavioral problems.

In this process of psychotherapy I listen to many stories that clients tell me about themselves and their beliefs. Generally their stories reflect some misconceptions or other dysfunctional thoughts about life—often thoughts that they have not put into words, thoughts that are not conscious. I can think of many examples, but one in particular quickly comes to mind. I had a client who believed that something bad was going to happen to her, and she was experiencing greater and greater anxiety as time went by, believing that this "bad thing" was going to happen soon. This belief, though, was not conscious; that is, she had not voiced it, at least not for some years. But by accessing her unconscious thoughts through hypnosis, she became aware of her belief. She recalled that when she was young her aunt told her that her life so far had been good, but life does not remain good, and that something bad would eventually happen to her. With this recollection she realized that for many years she had carried this belief deep within her, a belief that was not necessarily true. Through hypnosis, a deeper life story arose, a story that needed to be rewritten.

Some people may think that it might be easy to change such a life story by just not thinking it, but that is not the case. The belief had resided in her unconscious mind for much of her life; it was her natural way of thinking. As we will see later in this book in the case studies detailed in chapters 3, 4, and 5, willpower is not sufficient to change deeply engrained, reflexive thinking. One school of psychotherapy, cognitive behavioral therapy (CBT), suggests that if you rewrite the belief—for example, "There is no reason why my life cannot continue to be great"—and then repeat this new belief over and over again to yourself, it will eventually take up residence in your unconscious mind, replacing the dysfunctional belief. In the language of CBT the new belief will then become automatic. While there is some truth to this technique of CBT, it is usually not quite this easy.

Hypnosis can be a much more powerful tool to help someone change a deep-seated belief. Around 1920, French-Swiss psychoanalyst Charles Baudouin offered several "laws of hypnosis," the third being the law of reversed effort. This states that "when an idea imposes itself on the mind to such an extent as to give rise to a suggestion, all the conscious efforts which the subject makes in order to counteract this suggestion are not merely without the desired effect, but they actually run counter to the subject's conscious wishes and tend to intensify the suggestion."[1] This kind of negative self-hypnosis was more recently restated by psychologist

Daniel Araoz: "It is not will-power (left-hemispheric functioning) that produces change but imagination (right-hemispheric functioning). Conscious effort of the will is useless as long as the imagination is adverse to that effort."[2] While in trance the imagination is triggered and can override the negative beliefs by using statements like "Let your adult self go back and be with your younger self when your younger self first heard that bad things happen in life, and let your adult self reassure your younger self that this negative belief is not necessarily true, and that waiting for something bad to happen is a waste of time." In the case of the woman mentioned above, this was the beginning of a new personal story to be learned by her. The hypnotic techniques of psychotherapy, and more specifically analytic hypnotherapy, are well described, with a number of case studies, in my first book, *Grendel and His Mother.*

THE TRANCE STATE

What is trance? It is a less critical, more focused, yet altered state of consciousness. The various forms of meditation, dreaming while sleeping, hypnosis, and ecstatic trance are all altered states of consciousness, each with its own differences and similarities. One aspect that all these altered states have in common is that each is a way of sidestepping the incessant thoughts of our conscious mind, thoughts that interfere with seeing beyond that which we call "rational" thinking. Rational thinking depends on sensory input from our recognized five senses: sight, sound, taste, smell, and touch. Trance takes us into an extrasensory world, a world beyond our senses, connecting us with our unconscious mind and beyond, to what has been variously called the *collective unconscious,* the *universal mind,* the *Akashic field,* the *morphic field,* and the *divine matrix.*

We've all experienced trance. Have you ever gone to a movie and when it's over you leave the theater feeling a brief sense of confusion, as in, "It's still light out? Where did I park the car?" This feeling tells you that you were in a trance while watching the movie. Or if you are talking with a friend and what seems like ten minutes turns out to be an hour, you are in a trance. As a therapist I have learned how to lead a person into such a trance. This is done primarily through what psychologists call the *yes-set,* which will be described in more detail in the next chapter. By using trance, whether hypnotic or ecstatic, to sidestep the thoughts that interfere with the stories our unconscious mind tells us, these stories can be accessed. Connecting with these automatic stories that we may not be able to put into words brings us closer to the solutions of the problems that arise from these stories.

These trance stories are often in a different language, the language of metaphor such as what we experience in our nighttime dreams. Metaphor is a shortcut way of organizing experiences, a way of relating different yet similar experiences through analogies. Also, the logic of these stories is different from rational logic, such as the rational deduction that *B* is caused by *A,* or that *B* follows *A.* In contrast, the logic within the trance state, whether it occurs in dreaming, hypnosis, or ecstatic trance, may be free of causality and time. In other words, in trance, *B* may cause *A,* or *B* may come before *A* or at the same time as *A.* Rational causality and order are lost and become time-free and transparent while in trance.

Like various forms of trance, a dream is another altered state of consciousness. For some people dreams are meaningless, random images; to others they are divine revelations. From my own experience dreams are revelations from the unconscious that reflect the struggles of life, whether from the struggles between the parts of the self or from the struggles that result from relationships. They deal with life traumas, whether current or past, and provide direction for becoming self-actualized. Dreams clarify and reflect the struggles of dealing with changes in life and can be of great use as benchmarks for tracking the progress of change in the course of therapy.

SOUL RETRIEVAL

Some people who experience ecstatic trance for the first time are disappointed by the shallow or limited nature of their experience. However, hypnotic verbal suggestions, when used along with the induction ritual of ecstatic trance (described later in this chapter), can bring the person into a deeper and fuller ecstatic experience. Then, with this initial experience being deeper and fuller, subsequent experiences with ecstatic trance will likely be deeper and fuller as well, at first with fewer, and then finally no verbal suggestions necessary. This hybrid process leads a person to experience ecstatic trance with greater personal rewards.

Hypnosis has generally been taught as a collection of hypnotic therapeutic techniques separate from any specific model of psychotherapy. In this book, hypnosis will be used sparingly, as a bridge for teaching ecstatic trance and as an integral part of narrative psychotherapy to help people overcome their compulsive behavior, obsessive thoughts, and other behavioral and emotional problems. The hypnotic suggestions in this book might include statements like "You are capable of change and growth," "You are strong and ready to face feared tormentors" (an ego-strengthening statement), or "You face these tormentors with an attitude of patience, curiosity, wonder, and openness" (referring to such tormentors that become the building blocks for an "affect bridge," the bridge between the feelings or affect caused by the tormentor and the forgotten or unconscious source of when and how this pattern of emotional torment was learned earlier in life).[3] While facing these tormentors, hypnotic age regression is used on our journey into the unconscious mind to uncover early childhood experiences, the source of the dysfunctional thoughts and beliefs that sustain our compulsive dysfunctional behaviors.[4] Such hypnotic imagery techniques as having the adult self go back and be with the younger self are used to help the person understand the content of the journey.[5]

Along with uncovering dysfunctional ways of thinking, hypnotic trance, as well as ecstatic trance, is a strategy that can facilitate desired changes. Hypnotic imagery reframes beliefs, facilitates dialogue between ego states, and brings about the death of the dysfunctional beliefs and the birth of innocence, wherein healthy thinking becomes automatic and unconscious. These strategies and suggestions are verbal in nature, and though used initially in ecstatic trance as a way to teach the person to go into a deeper trance, the amount of such verbal suggestion rapidly diminishes over the course of therapy as the therapeutic direction is provided by the ecstatic postures used. This process of the death of dysfunctional beliefs and the birth of healthy innocence is referred to as *soul retrieval*.

Note that the language of this book is frequently in first person plural—*we, us,* and *our*—because we as therapists need to experience this journey of soul retrieval ourselves to be able to identify with it and follow it in the journeys of our clients.

WHAT IS ECSTATIC TRANCE?

Many people are familiar with hypnotic trance, which is induced by the therapist through slow and quiet speech that is paced to the person's rate of breathing. This technique usually invokes the aforementioned yes-set. In brief, the yes-set works by the therapist setting up a repetitive pattern of statements that elicit "yes, that's correct" responses, which gets the client into a habitual response. The answer of "yes, that's correct" is generally nonverbal as it is said to one's self, but as the therapist I often see a slight nod of the head or a slowing of breathing rate that tells me that my statement did reflect the experience of the client. Once the pattern is established and the person automatically answers "yes," then the question that you really want the "yes" to is slipped in.[6]

Ecstatic trance differs from hypnotic trance in that it is not invoked through these kinds of verbal suggestions, but rather by stimulating the nervous system through the rapid beating of a drum or the shaking of a rattle and the use of specific body postures. In fact, Felicitas Goodman, who pioneered the form of ecstatic trance journeying covered in this book, identified five conditions necessary for inducing ecstatic trance: (1) the belief that the experience is normal, enjoyable, and pleasurable; (2) a private, sacred physical space; (3) a meditative technique to quiet the mind; (4) rhythmic stimulation of the nervous system; and (5) specific body postures that provide different effects on the trance experience.[7]

From these necessary conditions, Goodman developed a ritual to induce ecstatic trance. Initially both the induction ritual and the posture are explained to the person, including time for questions and answers, so that participants can become familiar with the process.[8] Along with demonstrating the specific ecstatic posture to be used in the trance session, the idea that the experience is normal, enjoyable, and pleasurable is instilled in participants. Then the induction ritual is performed: the sacred or private physical space is defined by means of smudging with herbal smoke as an act of cleansing one's aura and the space where the ritual will be performed and then calling the spirits of each direction. These two acts define the private space. To meet the condition of a meditative technique to quiet the mind, participants are instructed to pay attention to their breathing for five minutes while sitting, lying down, or standing in a comfortable position. All this sets the stage for the ecstatic trance induction, which occurs by stimulating the nervous system rhythmically by means of beating a drum or shaking a rattle at a rate of approximately 210 beats per minute. During the fifteen minutes of drumming or rattling, participants assume the specified ecstatic posture.

Goodman found in the ancient and contemporary art of hunting and gathering cultures of the world the postures that she believed were used by their healers and shamans.[9] She discovered that certain body postures produce different experiences. These experiences fall into seven basic categories: (1) healing; (2) divination; (3) journeying into the underworld, (4) the middle world, or (5) the upper world; (6) initiation, or death and rebirth; and (7) metamorphosis, or shape-shifting. The first time I experimented with the ecstatic trance postures, at a workshop at the 2007 conference of the International Association for the Study of Dreams, I was very much impressed with their power to produce these specific experiences. I have since continued my trance work with these postures and to date have collected several thousand experiences from participants in my various ecstatic trance groups.

Felicitas Goodman's Discovery of the Ecstatic Trance Postures

Felicitas Goodman was born in Hungary and educated in Germany in linguistics. She learned and spoke approximately twenty languages and became valued as a scientific translator. Upon coming to the United States, her abilities in scientific translation made her valuable on college campuses. While at Ohio State University she met anthropologist Erika Bourguignon, who was studying ecstatic trance in 486 small societies. Goodman took an interest in Bourguignon's research and decided to pursue a graduate degree in anthropology, studying ecstatic trance. This interest led her to Mexico to study the form of ecstatic trance that brought about glossolalia—speaking in tongues—in the Mayan- and Spanish-speaking Apostolic churches there. One conclusion of her research was that there was no linguistic difference in the glossolalia of people whose native language was Spanish or Mayan. But her other consideration was to determine the factors that led a person to the ecstatic trance experience of speaking in tongues. While immersing herself in the rituals of these churches, Goodman determined that there were four necessary conditions for bringing about this ecstatic trance experience, one fewer than the five described above: (1) the belief that the experience is normal, enjoyable, and pleasurable; (2) a private physical space; (3) a meditative technique to quiet the mind; and (4) rhythmic stimulation of the nervous system.

By now Goodman had started teaching at Denison University, in Ohio, so upon returning to her students at Denison she developed a secular, more indigenous ritual that incorporated these four elements. She started by first discussing with participants what was expected from the ecstatic trance, portraying it as normal, enjoyable, and pleasurable. She then defined the private physical space by means of smudging and calling the spirits. This was followed by quieting the mind by focusing on breathing. Finally she induced ecstatic trance in the participants by stimulating the nervous system with the rapid beating of a drum or the shaking of a rattle.

Goodman found that this ritual was fairly effective in inducing ecstatic trance, but the experience did not quite meet her expectations. Sometime later she read an article by V. F. Emerson, a Canadian psychologist who was researching the effects of body postures on a number of physical variables of a person in meditation.[10] These variables included body temperature, breathing rate, skin moisture, and bowel motility. This research gave Goodman an idea that led her to begin her search of the literature and museum artifacts from around the world to find what she believed were the postures used by the shamans of hunter-gatherer cultures. She identified approximately fifty postures, which she used in rituals with her students and found that these postures induced the seven previously mentioned experiences in the ecstatic trance state. In this way Goodman added the use of specific body postures to her list of the four needed conditions to induce a meaningful ecstatic trance experience.

THE INDUCTION RITUAL: CALLING THE SPIRITS

Calling the spirits is an especially powerful and intrinsic aspect of creating a private, sacred space in which to induce ecstatic trance. My way of calling them is to first call the spirits of the East: "Spirits of the East, of dawn, of spring, of the beginning of new life, we honor you; bring us your wisdom and join us." With these words I offer to the East a pinch of blue cornmeal. Then: "Spirits of the South, of the warmth of the middle of day, of summer, and of growth, we honor you. Bring us your wisdom and join us." Again, this request is accompanied with the offering of a pinch of cornmeal. Then the spirits of the West are called with a pinch of cornmeal: "Spirits of the West, of the sunset and of autumn, of the harvest and the productive years of life, we honor you. Bring us your wisdom and join us." This is followed by calling the spirits of the North, again with a pinch of cornmeal: "Spirits of the North, of nighttime and winter, of hibernation, dormancy, sleep, and death in preparation for a new birth at spring, we honor you. Bring us your wisdom and join us." Then we turn to the directions above and below, beginning with the heavens, the cosmos, offering a pinch of cornmeal: "Spirits of the universe, the universe that placed Earth in a position with respect to its Sun that sustains life, a relationship that determines the seasons, the cycle of night and day and of the tides of the oceans, we honor you. Bring us your wisdom and join us." And finally, in calling the spirits of our great Earth Mother with a pinch of cornmeal: "Spirits of the Earth, of all life and substances of the Earth that are interdependent, that sustain all life, we honor you. Bring us your wisdom and join us."

This litany is obviously Earth-oriented. Ecotheologian Thomas Berry recognized that the long-held belief that we are a superior species with dominion over the Earth places us in a position to be the destroyers of the Earth. To become one with the Earth we must give up this superior attitude and realize that we are just one small piece in the interdependency of everything. Our survival depends on everything of the Earth, a belief that we need to relearn to prevent our destruction of Earth and, in the process, ourselves. We are not the culmination of evolution but one small step in the continued evolution of life on Earth. Berry suggests that regaining this understanding of our place on Earth is reached in "the dreamworld that unfolds within us in our sleep, or in those visionary moments that seize upon us in our waking hours," as well as by regaining our "shamanic personality."[11] These altered states of consciousness in pursuit of oneness with Mother Earth are just what I have been seeking in the practice of ecstatic trance journeying.

THE POSTURES

Felicitas Goodman, in her 1990 book *Where the Spirits Ride the Wind,* presents approximately fifty ecstatic postures, though since publication of her book many more postures have been revealed. The book you are reading now, *Ecstatic Soul Retrieval,* uses only five postures, yet the power of these five postures, when used regularly in the process of ecstatic therapy, reinforces their effectiveness. They compose an outline for the therapeutic process of analytic hypnotherapy, though in the context of shamanism this may be referred to as *soul retrieval.*

The Bear Spirit Posture

The Bear Spirit is a healing posture, one that brings healing energy into the person's body. Here, as far as its application to the psychotherapeutic process, we diverge slightly from Goodman's use of this posture, which is used for healing during the fifteen-minute period of drumming. In a therapy setting (as well as in my ecstatic trance groups), however, we have found its special power when using it for about five minutes during the induction ritual, to quiet the mind.

In this posture, with our hands resting on our abdomen, we can feel our abdomen rising and falling with each breath when breathing correctly, from the diaphragm. This place where the hands rest is below the umbilicus and is the place I like to call the *center of harmony*. It is also known as the *dan t'ien* in tai chi. With each breath we feel a calming strength flowing into our body, and as we exhale, this calming strength flows throughout our body, calming our mind and increasing our ego strength to help us face our struggles in life with a clear and calm mind.

When I first began using this posture as part of the induction ritual, my ecstatic trance instructor, Belinda Gore, suggested that we ask permission of the Bear Spirit to use it in this way. Our group asked permission, and it was granted by the spirit. In therapy each person soon learns that it provides a calm increase of ego strength, a psychological term that refers to a person's capacity to maintain his or her own identity despite psychological pain, distress, turmoil, and conflict between internal forces as well as the demands of reality. The Bear Spirit is generally used in this way in one of the first sessions of therapy.

The Bear Spirit was first found among the coastal Kwakiutl people of the Pacific Northwest, but it has since been found in almost every culture around the world. In fact, it is probably the one posture found most frequently all over the world and has become the logo of the Cuyamungue Institute. (I have in my collection of ecstatic figurines two wooden figures from the San Blas Indians of Panama standing in this posture.)

Bear Spirit Posture

Stand with your feet parallel, about six inches apart, with toes forward and knees not locked but slightly flexed. Rest your hands, relaxed, on your abdomen, with the tips of your thumbs lightly touching each other above the navel and with your fingers bent such that the first knuckles of your index fingers touch each other below the navel, forming a triangle around your navel. Rest your elbows easily at your sides. Close your eyes, and gently tip your head back, as though you are looking at a point where the wall meets the ceiling.

Lady of Cholula Posture

Sit in a chair with your legs apart and your feet pointed straight ahead. Cup your left hand around the front of your left knee. Rest your right hand palm down with the fingers forward on your right leg, just above the knee and slightly to the right. Your left arm should be somewhat tensed as it is pulled forward, while your right arm is more relaxed. Depending on the height of the chair and the length of your legs it may be necessary to put a cushion under your feet to raise them so you can clasp your knee. Lean forward slightly, with your spine straight, hinging forward from the hips. Hold your head straight with your eyes closed but directed looking under your eyelids. Your tongue should protrude gently from between your lips.

The Lady of Cholula Posture

The second posture we generally use in a therapeutic setting is the Lady of Cholula. This figure was found in Cholula, Mexico; it is pre-Columbian, dating from around 1350 AD. She is sitting with a straight back at the edge of her seat, clasping her knees with her hand and wearing a conical hat. When we wear a facsimile of this headpiece in our practice it seems to intensify the experience, as if it is an antenna for receiving the answer to a question posed to the lady; thus she is a divination posture used to seek answers to our questions.

In sitting in the posture, the intent or feeling of it is that of alert anticipation—the anticipation of finding an answer to some question. The answer is often metaphorical and may not be quickly understood, but when the experience is returned to and held in awareness, the answer soon becomes evident, and it usually provides the beginning direction of therapy. The question is asked in a very general way; for example, "What do I need to be working on in therapy?" or "In what direction does my therapy need to move?" At other times it may be much more specific to the current situation, but in either case, the response gives direction.

The Jivaro Underworld Posture

The third posture, the Jivaro Underworld (or Lower World) posture, is used for journeying into the underworld of the unconscious mind.

This posture was found among the Jivaro people of South America. This posture generally leads a person on a journey into the unconscious, often a very deep experience that requires the ego strength offered initially by the Bear Spirit posture. It is often used to take one back in time, to a childhood experience that was the beginning of some dysfunctional or negative way of thinking. It generally brings an understanding of the source of the problem being faced in therapy, or an understanding of what is needed to resolve the problem.

Jivaro Underworld Posture

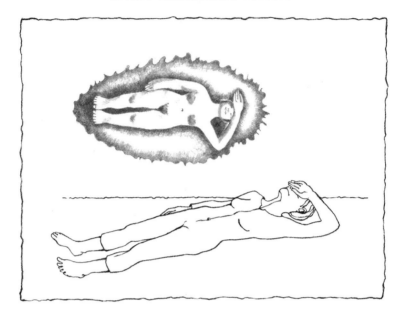

Lie on the floor (or a couch or reclining chair) with the back of your head resting comfortably on the floor. Bring your right arm beside your body in a natural, relaxed position. Raise your left arm, with the back of your left hand resting on the middle of your forehead, without any pressure on the eyes.

The Feathered Serpent Posture

This is an initiation or death-rebirth posture that brings about the death of the old way of thinking and the birth of a healthy and more functional way of thinking. The Feathered Serpent is the Mayan god of creation, with wings to carry it into the heavens and, as a serpent, to creep along on the ground. This particular figure dates from 100 to 650 AD and was found in Zacatecas, Mexico. The figurine is currently in the Los Angeles County Museum of Natural History. The figure is of a person standing erect, with the back of each hand resting on the hips.

Feathered Serpent Posture

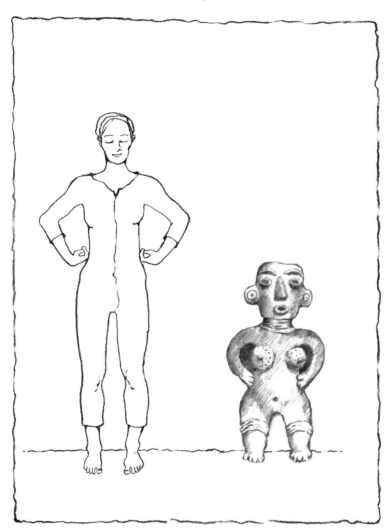

Stand with your feet parallel, about six inches apart, knees lightly bent, toes pointing straight forward. Cup your hands, and place them at your sides at waist level, with fingers curling upward and your arms rounded outward with bent elbows pointing to either side. Direct your face straight ahead, and close your eyes. Allow your mouth to open slightly.

When asked, "What does this posture express?" as you stand with the backs of your hands resting on your hips and elbows extending to either side, the answer is generally "determination"—a determination to let go of some negative way of thinking or believing and the birth of a more functional way of thinking.

The Olmec Prince Posture

In our process of ecstatic trance therapy, animal spirit guides are important for providing direction for change. At such times a shape-shifting posture may be valuable. The one I usually choose is the Olmec Prince.

The Olmec Prince was found in La Cruz del Milagro, Veracruz, Mexico. It dates from 800 to 300 BC and is now in the Museum of Anthropology in Jalapa, Mexico. When sitting in this posture you ask, "What is the intent of this posture?" to which the quick answer is, "to become a four-legged animal." The knuckles of your hands rest on the floor in front of you, which makes them feel like forelegs, yet in this posture I have also become a snake, a tree, and even a bird. The Olmec Prince is the first posture I ever used, and the first time I used it I became a high-stepping parade horse, and the second time I used it I became a bear.

Thus, of the seven main categories of ecstatic trance postures delineated by Felicitas Goodman—healing; divination; journeying into the underworld, the middle world, and the upper world; metamorphosis or shape-shifting; and initiation or death-rebirth—all can be used in the process of psychotherapy except two: journeying into the middle world and journeying into the upper world. There are a number of different postures for each of these seven categories of trance experiences, and the different postures within a category offer subtle differences in the trance experience. But in the process of ecstatic therapy only five postures, one from each of five categories of the seven, are used. These five are the ones I have found to be most effective and suitable to the therapeutic setting.

Ecstatic trance should be introduced gradually to those who come

Olmec Prince Posture

Sit on the floor with your right leg crossed in front of your left leg. (If this position is difficult for you, use pillows or yoga blocks for support.) Stretch your arms, with elbows locked, straight in front of you, with your fingers curled inward, toward your body, such that only the middle segment of each finger rests on the floor. Your shoulders, elbows, wrists, and knuckles are held rigid. To maintain this position you will need to lean slightly forward with your back straight, hinging from the hips. Lift your head with your closed eyes directed forward. Let your tongue protrude slightly from between your lips.

to psychotherapy, because many of the concepts of ecstatic trance could be foreign to one's expectations of therapy and might be seen as a threat to one's belief system. These five postures are sufficient for the process; introducing clients to more postures than this would take them beyond what they expect of therapy and be a distraction to their immediate needs in therapy. As gains occur in a person's personal growth, to achieve higher levels of maturity through this process of ecstatic therapy, and as the client sees the power of ecstatic trance to provide structure for this kind of growth, the person becomes more prepared to see beyond any limited personal expectations. At the end of ecstatic trance therapy I usually invite my clients to join my ecstatic trance posture group, where they are more prepared to experience and learn from a much broader range of available postures.

2

Adapting Ecstatic Trance to Psychotherapy

Coyote as trickster can be useful in generating a healing surprise, a shock that moves a patient from habitual state of illness into another, more precarious one, from whence he or she can "fall" into wellness.

LEWIS MEHL-MADRONA

Behind emotional and behavioral problems are ineffective, self-defeating, and negative beliefs. People come to psychotherapy because of these problems, and they tell their stories. I listen to these stories, in particular listening for the self-defeating and ineffective beliefs. Because of the emotional pain these beliefs cause they are frequently lost in myriad excuses, rationalizations, and distortions. These persistent, problematic beliefs are buried in the unconscious mind, inaccessible, but there they continue to directly affect the person's emotions and behavior. The dysfunctional beliefs are sometimes not in the form of words but in the form of mental images that come forward in dreams and trance experiences; they are either learned preverbally, are emotionally repressed because of their painful nature, or are learned during a formative stage of development without the application of critical thought.

People are most likely not aware of the connection between their limiting, self-defeating beliefs and their behavioral and emotional problems, but the unconscious beliefs need to be uncovered and revised or reframed in order for real change to occur. For example, why does the man with an explosive temper excuse himself by saying, "I can't let anybody take advantage of me!" As we will see in the case study in chapter 4, in his adolescence, when picked on by the school bully, he said to himself—and thus still says to himself—*If I don't defend myself, others will laugh at me.* These unconscious or semiconscious connections to early life experiences can be brought to awareness quite directly by hypnotically leading the sufferer back through time with the hypnotic suggestion to carry the problematic feeling back in time. Similarly, as I have discovered, the power of an ecstatic divination posture, along with the use of an ecstatic underworld posture that accesses the unconscious mind, can just as effectively produce results that are similar to what can be achieved by using the more conventional tools of psychotherapy.

THE PSYCHOTHERAPEUTIC ELEMENTS OF ECSTATIC TRANCE

For years in my work as a psychotherapist I favored the techniques of hypnotic age regression and the affect bridge of carrying one's feelings back through time in order to take a client back to the source of his or her unconscious beliefs, to the early, deep, and formative stories that direct the person's life.[1] Identifying these early experiences is necessary to help determine alternative, healthier ways of thinking that can help the client let go of the dysfunctional thoughts and images. However, over the years I have come to recognize that identifying the underlying stories and determining healthier alternatives can be accomplished through the ecstatic postures and ecstatic trance work with less of the kind of verbal direction that is required by hypnotic suggestion. When these dysfunctional beliefs become evident, whether they arise in dreams, hypnotic experiences, or ecstatic trance journeying, they can be considered more central, more honest, and clearer statements with regard to the person's problem. They immediately take us to the source of the problem and offer a deeper level of story by accessing the unconscious mind. Unveiling these deeper stories lays the groundwork for a deeper level of psychotherapy.

Of the many approaches to psychotherapy, I have primarily used hypnosis, dream work, and narrative therapy in my professional work. With regard to hypnosis, the school I primarily use is analytical hypnotherapy, which has a number of similarities to cognitive behavioral therapy (CBT), although the cognitive behavioral therapist would most likely disagree with me on this, and I will soon show why. CBT, hypnosis, and narrative therapy are all relevant to ecstatic trance therapy.

Cognitive Behavioral Therapy

Some readers may recognize certain similarities between ecstatic trance therapy and CBT. In fact, a number of writers have made just this comparison and would call ecstatic trance therapy a constructivist approach (one of constructing or reconstructing the early source of the dysfunctional belief) to CBT, as compared to the objectivist approach that says that change only happens in the here and now—an approach advocated by American psychiatrist Aaron Beck, considered the father of cognitive therapy.[2] What I call ineffective or dysfunctional thoughts, Beck calls automatic thoughts. "Automatic thoughts just happen, as if by reflex," he says, and the person accepts these thoughts as valid, "without question and without testing."[3]

The basic tenet of CBT is that once a person's dysfunctional automatic thinking is determined, this automatic thinking needs to be replaced with functional or healthy thinking. The person practices the new way of thinking until it is learned and becomes automatic. My experience is that simple practice is not sufficient to effect change because willpower alone is not sufficient. As mentioned in the previous chapter, willpower is a left-hemisphere function, while imagination is a right-hemisphere function. At times, when a person practices behaviorally the new way of thinking (left hemisphere), some life experience may occur to deeply and emotionally (right hemisphere) reinforce the negative way of thinking, thus the new way of thinking is blocked by the more powerful imagination. Yet at other times life experiences may be seen as reinforcing the new way of thinking, allowing it to become automatic. I believe that making the new thinking automatic is more ensured when using hypnotic trance to bring the new thinking and images into the realm of the unconscious mind. The CBT practitioner, however, denies or does not believe in the usefulness of the concept of the unconscious mind.

A second area of disagreement between CBT and ecstatic trance therapy involves the need to go back in time to consider the source of the problem. Whereas the constructionist recognizes the power of hypnotic or ecstatic age regression to take the person back to early childhood experiences, this approach is not considered important in the objectivist approach to CBT.[4] The objectivist, believing that change occurs only in the here and now, would say that one does not need to dwell on the past, and that dwelling on the past, as in Freudian psychoanalysis, is a waste of time. However, the experiences from the past that arise from analytic hypnotherapy and dream work are not the focus of prolonged attention as in the process of psychoanalysis but are simply used to bridge (the "affect bridge") or to make a connection to the present problems and to provide some understanding as to why these dysfunctional beliefs continue to be held.

This process of therapy to overcome the disorders of behavior and emotions is cognitive and often behavioral, but the constructionist approach as well as the narrative approach diverge from the expectations of objectivist-oriented CBT in that both unconscious processes and past experiences are considered important.[5] Because the objectivist CBT practitioner depreciates or denies the concept of the unconscious, dream work has played only a very minor role in CBT. Nevertheless, I believe that with continued efficacy research in CBT, the barrier put up by CBT practitioners and researchers in devaluing the unconscious will eventually fall away, and both hypnosis and dream work, as well as ecstatic trance, will become tools of CBT.

Analytical Hypnotherapy

As we will see later in our case studies, integrating ecstatic trance into the process of psychotherapy initially requires a hybrid approach in which the concept underlying ecstatic trance is introduced by using various hypnotic suggestions.

What is hypnosis and what are these hypnotic suggestions? Hypnosis, an altered state of consciousness, is where the client feels a deep sense of validation from and rapport with the therapist. This validation and rapport are attained through hypnotic suggestions that take the form of a yes-set.[6] As described in the previous chapter, a yes-set is a mental set of answering "yes" to suggestions made by the therapist, while the therapist's words accurately recognize what the client is experiencing. For example, if the client is leaning back against the back of a chair, a beginning yes-set suggestion might be, "As you sit, feel the warmth on your back as it rests against the back of the chair." This comment, something for which the client answers to him- or herself, "Yes, that's right," might be an early comment in inducing trance. If the client were wearing jeans, I might suggest, "Feel the roughness and tightness of your jeans as they press against your knees." As this hypnotic, yes-set language continues, the suggestions become more relevant to the client's feelings and emotions that he or she brought to therapy; for example, "You are feeling a lot of anxiety that your wife might leave you because of your anger" or "It is very depressing that your job feels so meaningless."

Some clients come to therapy with the expectation and request that I use hypnosis. I have become well known in the area for my use of hypnosis. With these clients, to meet their expectation, I will use a more formal induction procedure beginning with statements like, "Sit back, close your eyes, and relax as I lead you into a state of trance." The language of the "yes-set" has become so much a part of my language that even those who are not expecting the use of hypnosis will often fall into a state of trance. I use this same language when adding ecstatic postures, which allows the client to quickly and easily attain a trance state.

As the client's answer of "yes" becomes a habit, suggestions that may be helpful to the person can become more divergent from his or her reality; for example, as an exercise I suggest, "Take your feeling of anxiety back through time, and as you see the time go by, days, months, seasons, years, something in your life will stand out and catch your attention. When this something catches your attention, lift the index finger of your left hand [or another finger visible to me]." After a while the finger lifts (considered ideomotor signaling, a common technique in analytic hypnotherapy), and I can then ask, "What are you experiencing now?" As previously mentioned, this process of taking a feeling back through time is the affect bridge. In the state of trance, taking the feeling back through time takes it back to when it was first experienced early in life. This process may be repeated several times in the course of a session in order to take the person back to the original incident that triggered the anxiety or feeling of concern.

Facing these early life experiences can be fearful, so suggestions to increase a person's ego strength are important. One such hypnotic suggestion is: "Each day in every way you feel stronger and stronger." However, this same ego strength can be attained quite efficiently, without the lengthy verbal suggestions required by analytical hypnotherapy, by using the Bear Spirit posture of standing tall and feeling a calming, strengthening energy entering your center of harmony, that place below your umbilicus where your hands rest. The simple fact that the person has come in for psychotherapy is already a sign that she has attained a sufficient degree of emotional strength to face these more fearful experiences.

Next, hypnosis with the affect bridge is used to carry the troublesome emotion back in time to its source. To accomplish this age regression, such hypnotic language as, "As you sit and relax let the days, months, years pass by as you carry the feeling of anxiety (or other pertinent feeling) back through time." This is repeated slowly at the rate of the client's breathing. I soon add the suggestion that "when you come to a place in time that especially catches your attention, lift your finger." This is also repeated occasionally until the person's finger lifts. Then I request that the person report on what he is experiencing. The same results can be attained while sitting in the Lady of Cholula posture by simply requesting of the Lady of Cholula to take the person back to when he or she first felt the anxiety without the extensive and repetitive verbal instructions of analytical hypnotherapy to bring about a regression in age.

Upon going back to an earlier age with this awareness of the initial incident that brought about the troublesome feelings, another hypnotic suggestion can be made: "Let your adult self go back and be with your younger self and help your younger self understand." This suggestion brings the source of the problem to a greater sense of conscious awareness and leads the person to explore and discover the irrationality and ineffectiveness of the feelings and way of thinking. So using the example found in the previous chapter of the woman who learned at a young age that "life is good now, but you need to expect that something bad will eventually happen," I might suggest, "Let your adult self go back and be with your younger self, and with all the wisdom and understanding of your adult self let your younger self realize that something bad does not have to happen, and waiting for it to happen is a waste of time." This can lead the person to a deeper sense of discovery and the beginning of the path toward resolution. When experienced in a state of hypnotic trance, the new belief is more directly carried into the realm of the unconscious mind. Lying in the Jivaro Underworld posture can increase the efficiency of this process of journeying in the unconscious mind.

The new healthier way of thinking is then reinforced with such hypnotic suggestions as, "Let your adult self go back and be with your younger self to find the right words to help your younger self." For example, this same woman might say to herself, "I can look forward to the positive things that will continue to happen in my life." Another example of this would be someone who carries his or her depression or anxiety back to abuse inflicted by the father at an early age. A suggestion that can begin the process of healing would be, "Let your adult self go back and be with your younger self and help your younger self find the words to say what you need." The response might be, "Dad, I need you to be gentle," or "Dad, I need you to be sensitive to my feelings," or "Mom, I need you to protect me from Dad." These needs can be expressed in many ways and should be expressed in as many ways as possible, always in the positive language of what is needed, not in negative terms such as "Dad, I need you to not be abusive." Negative language does not offer what is needed and leaves a void.

This third step in the process of analytic hypnotherapy is reflected in the hypnotic language of, "Become the good, gentle, and understanding dad, the healthy dad, and the protective mom in your relationships with your children and with others in your life." This language brings about the death of the hopeless feelings ingrained in childhood, the feelings of not knowing what to do, and the birth of a new and healthier self, of becoming the healthy father and mother to oneself and others. In terms of ecstatic trance work, this third step is a death-rebirth experience. Using the Feathered Serpent posture can bring the person to the same death-rebirth experience and can add to the effectiveness of the hypnotic suggestions (as shown above) by involving the person more totally in the experience.

In all three steps, analytic hypnotherapy requires that the client share the story of his or her life, whereas in using the ecstatic trance postures the story does not need to be revealed if such a revelation is uncomfortable to the person (though in the therapy session this is generally not the case). The hypnotic experience is generally just mental, just in the person's head, but by using an ecstatic trance posture, the person is more totally, physically involved in the process.

Narrative Therapy

In this form of psychotherapy clients come to each session with new stories about themselves to tell. Some stories arise from dreams, hypnosis, and ecstatic trance, stories that are from the unconscious and reveal deeper beliefs held by the person. The role of the therapist is to provide counternarratives to reframe the dysfunctional aspects of the client's stories. In this way therapy becomes a storytelling session. Stories are easily remembered. The stories heard in childhood are remembered, and so are the stories of adulthood. Whereas theoretical constructs are quickly forgotten, real stories of life and the teaching tales they embody can nudge a person along in a healthier direction. This is the advantage of narrative therapy.

Ecstatic healing is full of these stories, which arise during the ecstatic trance experience and can thus be considered a form of narrative therapy.

AWAKENING CONSCIOUSNESS THROUGH ECSTATIC TRANCE

David Korten, former faculty at Harvard School of Business, political activist, prominent critic of the "global suicide economy,"[7] and by training and inclination a student of psychology and behavioral systems, draws from a number of models of child development to extract the manner in which we relate to others as we mature. His book *The Great Turning: From Empire to Earth Community* describes the five stages of development that provide a template for assessing the progress toward greater maturity that a person makes in therapy.

The first stage of consciousness in our earliest years is magical. We fantasize new worlds around us and find protection in our magical warriors. As we grow out of this stage, we enter a period in which we seek power over our world. Korten calls this second stage "imperial consciousness,"[8] the stage of playing up to the powerful and exploiting the oppressed. He views those adults who are greedy, who seek the accumulation of wealth, and who measure their success in terms of their wealth as being stuck at this stage. It is a stage of self-centeredness and self-absorbency—the stage at which some people seek therapy to work out the problems that ensue when one is stuck at this level of development.

As these people find resolution of their immediate emotional pain, they can step beyond the stage of self-centeredness and begin to relate to and experience with greater rapport the feelings of those around them, their families, neighbors, and associates, offering understanding and accepting them for who they are. This third stage of development Korten calls "socialized consciousness," the stage in which we are seen as "good citizens."[9] At this stage we live in a small world, among those who think like us and reinforce our way of thinking. We play by the rules of our identity group, and from within this group we expect a fair reward. Korten sees these people as being the majority of adults. This group is the linchpin between the culture of empire and the culture of the Earth community.

Those who develop beyond this stage of socialized consciousness into the fourth stage of development Korten calls "cultural creatives."[10] These people are capable of living in a world inclusive of others who may think differently from them, and yet they identify with life-affirming societies that work for the good of all. *Cultural creatives* is a term that was originally coined by sociologist Paul H. Ray and psychologist Sherry Ruth Anderson to describe people whose values embrace a curiosity and concern for the world, its ecosystem, and its people, and who display an awareness of and activism on behalf of peace and social justice.[11] In their 2000 book *The Cultural Creatives,* Ray and Anderson claim to have found that 50 million adult Americans—a little over a quarter of the adult population—fit into this category.[12] When a person evolves in such a way as to seek to go beyond the world of like-minded people and in fact values the fact that there are differences among people, and that these differences are valuable, then he or she is on the road to becoming a cultural creative.

Finally, the most mature among us are those who have attained the fifth stage of development, that of spiritual consciousness. Korten calls these people "spiritual creatives," those who live in a complex and evolving world in which they engage as evolutionary co-creators. They are the elders in this new integral world that recognizes the interdependency of all things of the Earth. It is only from this position of spiritual consciousness that we can lead others in their personal growth to higher levels of maturity. To enter this new world as an elder, a teacher of others, is to enter a world well beyond the goal of conventional psychotherapy; however, this fifth stage of development is fostered by the ongoing practice of ecstatic trance, especially if done with a group of people who also practice ecstatic trance.

So to borrow from Korten, the goals of psychotherapy are met when the client becomes a good citizen living in the world of socialized consciousness; as well, the expectations of insurance companies are satisfied when people become good citizens in their narrow world of like-minded people. This is the majority of adults. However, the rituals of ecstatic trance look beyond this limited world of like-mindedness and seek to bring people to higher levels of maturity, to attain cultural consciousness and, ultimately, spiritual consciousness. When someone discovers the power of the ecstatic postures—postures that were found among hunter-gatherer cultures, cultures far different from the socialized consciousness favored by modern Western culture—the door opens for that person to discover the power of different peoples, different cultures, and perhaps even different time lines. This exploration helps to move the person into a bigger, more spacious, and higher consciousness.

The ecstatic trance induction ritual of calling the spirits of each direction introduces a person to the sense of interdependency with the Earth and all her elements and her cycles, and relating to an animal spirit guide through a metamorphosis posture opens one up to being able to relate to, and therefore value, other life-forms. At this level of consciousness, which is spiritual, one is better prepared to become an elder in the Earth community and a teacher of others. This level of maturity goes well beyond the expectations of psychotherapy. In fact, the conclusion of one or more rounds of ecstatic trance therapy, after the immediate problems have found resolution, the person is often ready and willing to explore beyond the scope of psychotherapy, to investigate their human potential. At this point I usually invite him or her to join our ecstatic trance group, where in a loving and diverse setting we all are working toward the ultimate aim of spiritual consciousness.

INTRODUCING ECSTATIC TRANCE INTO THERAPY

The five-part ritual of ecstatic trance as pioneered by Felicitas Goodman is more indigenous and shamanic and would seem to be quite foreign to most people who come to psychotherapy. For example, calling the spirits of each direction, part of the induction ritual, might seem odd in this setting, yet I have found that calling the spirits is especially powerful in the process of therapy and most important for personal growth beyond therapy. The challenge of this book has been to show how to bring the five necessary conditions for ecstatic trance journeying into the process of traditional psychotherapy so as to meet the expectations of the client. As with the use of analytic hypnotherapy, I continue to use the language of the yes-set throughout the therapy session. I generally do not initially introduce ecstatic trance and the ecstatic postures as a specific technique, but blend them into the therapy session. This adds to the effectiveness of the process by incorporating the person more completely through her posture.

Ecstatic trance work must be introduced gradually so as to fit appropriately within the client's expectations and at the right stage of therapy. For example, early on in therapy, when the person is struggling with personal problems, he or she is most likely not ready to understand of the importance of calling the spirits of the directions. Calling the spirits is considered appropriate only later in therapy, once the person can look beyond his or her personal, self-centered struggle and display concern for others and for their immediate community. However, once he or she is ready to embark on a deeper level of exploration, the induction ritual as delineated by Felicitas Goodman can be introduced. Meanwhile, at even the most basic level, most novices will be able to experience the immediate results of standing in the Bear Spirit posture for a few minutes, focusing on diaphragm breathing, to achieve a state of calmness.

As mentioned previously, a traditional ecstatic trance session is preceded by a preparatory stage in which there is a discussion of what to expect from ecstatic trance and answers to any questions. In using ecstatic postures in the psychotherapy setting, questions and discussion of the goals of therapy is natural but not necessarily directed specifically to ecstatic trance. The belief that the experience is normal, enjoyable, and pleasurable is easily reinforced by the results of the therapeutic exercises completed in trance.

The Induction Ritual

Of the five steps necessary to induce ecstatic trance (see pages 7–8), establishing a private sacred space is evident in the context of a session of psychotherapy in the therapy room itself, along with the assurance by the therapist of confidentiality. As mentioned above, the technique of calling on the spirits is omitted in early therapy sessions until the client is ready. Using postures, such as the Bear Spirit posture, is a natural way of focusing on one's breathing from the diaphragm, or center of harmony, and to relax as well as to increase one's ego strength for the work ahead. The two steps introduced early in therapy that might be considered odd are the rapid rhythmic stimulation to the nervous system and the bodily postures. With sufficient explanation these two elements are easily accepted. Usually in using hypnotic trance I have new age music playing quietly in the background to help in relaxation. With ecstatic trance I use recorded drumming that is quiet but rapid. I explain that the purpose of the drumming is to stimulate the nervous system with an energy that keeps the person alert to the therapeutic task at hand and serves to quell any competing and distracting thoughts that may arise. Finally, any one of the five ecstatic postures described in this book can feel natural in therapy provided it too is adequately explained as follows.

The Bear Spirit:
Relaxation and Ego-Strengthening

In analytic hypnotherapy the initial step to induce trance is a hypnotic exercise to teach the client to relax and increase ego strength for facing what may be uncovered in journeying into the unconscious mind. This need for increased ego strength exists because what will be uncovered is often painful or even frightening. This very same objective of increasing relaxation and strengthening one's ego can also be attained in ecstatic trance work by using the Bear Spirit posture, and this is what I tell my first-time ecstatic trance clients. Note that initially the actual name of the Bear Spirit posture is not used; the full explanation of the posture is reserved for later in therapy, after the client has experienced all four or five postures that are used in therapy. At that point the source of all the postures and their names are explained. We do this because we don't want the person to get too intellectual this early on in the process (left hemisphere) by having to absorb all this new information, which becomes a distraction or diversion from the immediacy of what is happening in the therapeutic process. As well, the person will appreciate this information more once the effectiveness of posture work is a visceral experience and the benefits are felt (right hemisphere) by the client. Thus the posture is taught as an integral part of a breathing exercise for relaxation such that giving it a name is not necessary.

The ecstatic trance induction ritual pioneered by Felicitas Goodman calls for the person to focus on his breathing to quiet the mind while sitting or lying in a comfortable position for about five minutes. In the psychotherapy setting with the sound of rapid drumming being played softly in the background, I explain to the client that breathing from the diaphragm is important for relaxation, especially when the client is experiencing chest tightness due to anxiety. The words and description I use are paced to his rate of breathing, and I continue to invoke the trance-inducing "yes-set." I often suggest that he watch a baby breathing if there is a baby in his life, noting how the baby is breathing from the abdomen rather than the chest. I will explain that a person's rigid rib cage inhibits a person's ability to breathe from the chest, thus causing the feeling of chest tightness. I will have him place his hands on his abdomen and feel his abdomen rise and fall as he breathes from the diaphragm. I offer the words, "As you inhale and your abdomen rises, feel a sense of strength and relaxation flow into your body, and as you exhale and your abdomen falls, feel the strength and relaxation spread throughout your body. Feel a sense of quietness as it fills your head." After repeating these words a couple of times, I will then stand and motion for the client to stand with me nodding to him to place his hands on his abdomen as I am demonstrating, standing straight with our shoulders back in a posture that brings about a sense of increased emotional strength. It is key that I, as the therapist, also stand in the posture: while standing with the client in the same posture I find that I frequently experience what the client is feeling and experiencing. We stand together in silence, with eyes closed, and breathe in this way for approximately five minutes, experiencing a sense of increased pleasurable strength. The place where the hands naturally rest in this posture is just below the navel, the dan t'ien as it is called in Tai Chi, the place I like to call the *center of harmony*. This focus naturally provides a sense of relaxing strength, a sense of inner peace, and the experience of harmony. This exercise is not only trance inducing but is a beneficial relaxation exercise for all clients. Because of its benefits, I use it regularly as an exercise early in therapy, often during the first session.

At the end of the session a recording of the drumming is given to the client along with the recommendation to practice this exercise frequently, at least once a day, at home. The gift of the recording serves as a bridge between the experience in the therapy room and the experience at home, increasing the depth and effectiveness of this exercise of relaxation, ego strengthening, and quieting the mind and providing the person with a valuable self-help tool.

This period of relaxation and ego strengthening is a learned response and requires some practice, but once learned it can easily be called on whenever needed. Over the next session or two my verbal suggestion of inhaling a sense of calmness and letting the calmness spread throughout the body as he exhales is gradually reduced and eventually eliminated altogether, as is the use of drumming during this short five-minute period of relaxation (though I suggest that he continue to use it at home). The drumming is then reserved for the fifteen minutes of trance using any of the other four ecstatic postures. After the person learns to relax with increased ego strength, all that is needed to relax and increase ego strength is to ask the person to stand tall for a few minutes with his hands on the center of harmony while breathing from the diaphragm.

The Lady of Cholula:
Seeking Answers to Questions

A session or two after this relaxation exercise is introduced is the time to introduce the Lady of Cholula divination posture. The therapist demonstrates the posture for the client, who is instructed to sit at the edge of the chair with hands clasping the knees, and then asks, "What do you think this posture expresses?" or "What are you feeling sitting in this posture?" Generally the answer is something to the effect of, "I am sitting attentively waiting for something." This posture is used to find answers to questions raised in therapy, so sitting in this way naturally feels like one is waiting attentively for an answer. The posture is likely repeated many times over the course of therapy, whenever there is a need to search for an answer from the unconscious mind or even the universal mind or collective conscious.

The first time this posture is used the intention is usually to find the source of the emotional problem that brought the person to therapy, so it might be voiced as, "What first caused my anxiety?" or "What first caused my depression?" Or it may be worded as a request: "Take me back to when I first was troubled with anxiety." These words are again paced to the person's breathing and quietly repeated several times throughout the fifteen minutes of trance while the drumming is playing quietly in the background.

This is an example of the affect bridge and occurs after the hypnotic suggestions for relaxation and ego strengthening are offered. The language is basically this: "Take with you the feeling of anxiety as you begin to go back through time. Watch the days, months, seasons, years go by as you go back through time. As you go back through time, watching time pass, soon some incident in your life will catch your attention. When this incident arises, lift the index finger of your left hand." This or similar language is repeated slowly, at the rate of the client's breathing. When the finger lifts the client is asked to relate the experience. This procedure may be repeated for going back even further in time. For example, the woman who was anxiously waiting for something bad to happen returned to the early experience of her aunt's telling her that life is not a bed of roses, bad things happen to people along the way. When the client lifts a finger and is asked to describe what is going on in her inner experience, the trance remains unbroken and is maintained because the soft drumming continues playing in the background. The continuation of trance allows the client to easily return to the trance journey to go back even further in time.

Using this hypnotic language along with the posture can more quickly bring the person to experience the intent of the posture, of finding the source of the troublesome behavior or emotion. Using the posture complements the hypnotic language by involving the whole person in discovering the affect bridge. With subsequent use of this posture in the course of therapy, the repetitiveness of the hypnotic words can decrease because the intent of such language is clearly reflected in the posture itself. Whereas with Goodman's method the ecstatic experience is not interrupted during the fifteen minutes of drumming, with this hybrid approach the person may interrupt the drumming to describe the experience. When the person is finished, she can return to the journey with the suggestion, "Let yourself go back further in time to an even earlier time when you first experienced your anxiety [or other emotion of concern]" to continue moving back in time. If the client interrupts the drumming to relate her experience, the drumming can still continue while she speaks, thereby helping her return to the trance journey. If the drumming stops while the client relates the experience, it may be turned back on to allow her to continue the journey. As with the Bear Spirit posture, I join the client in sitting in the Lady of Cholula posture, which facilitates empathy and allows me to experience what the client is experiencing. If the experience of going back in time feels complete, then one beneficial suggestion for ending the session might be, "Let the wisdom of your adult self go back and be with your younger self to help your younger self understand." If the experience has been metaphorically cryptic, this kind of direction may provide the person with an understanding of the cryptic language of the metaphor. As well, embedded in this experience are likely to be suggestions for resolving the person's problem. At first the solutions may be frightening because of the possible changes to the person's life, and the inclusion of the adult self is useful at this point. There are infinite variations on this suggestion, such that the right words can be found to match the particular problem brought to therapy.

The answer to the question, whether one is using the Lady of Cholula posture or is using analytic hypnotherapy, is generally in the language of imaginal metaphor. These images are important and are taken into the next step of therapy.

The Lady of Cholula figure was found in Cholula, Mexico, and is from the Mayan time period. However, providing this kind of background information is not done in therapy until the first four postures have been experienced and the process of ecstatic trance therapy is well underway.

The Jivaro Underworld Posture: Journeying into the Unconscious Mind

The next posture in the sequence used in therapy after the Lady of Cholula reveals what is to be carried into the underworld of the unconscious mind is the Jivaro posture. The explanation is offered that this posture is used for journeying into the "underworld" of the unconscious mind, an acceptable psychoanalytical construct. The use of the word *underworld* also feels quite natural in describing the intent of this posture. For this posture the client reclines on the couch with the wrist of the left hand resting on the forehead. Reclining on a couch in therapy is acceptable within the conventional model of therapy because this image is often portrayed in the practice in Freudian psychoanalysis, so this position does not feel so odd.

Once the Lady of Cholula posture has been introduced, at the next session I once again start out by having the client stand for a few minutes in the Bear Spirit posture. By now the relaxation, ego-strengthening, and mind quieting response gained from this posture has been learned and is triggered by the posture, so for these first few minutes nothing need be said, and the drumming is not used here but reserved for the underworld posture. Then as the drumming starts I instruct the client to recline on the couch and briefly offer a few words to remind her of the previous week's experience. (As with all the postures, I too take the posture, in this case lying back in my recliner.) For example, I might suggest, "Let your adult self go back and be with your younger self and help your younger self find the right words to express what you need from your aunt, to express the healthy way the early experience could have been handled." These instructions can be hypnotically repeated occasionally during the fifteen minutes and are likely to bring up more thoughts, so further discussion may occur.

For the woman who was anxiously waiting for something bad to happen, the words her unconscious mind needed to hear were, "Bad things do not necessarily have to happen. Waiting for something bad to happen is a waste of time." I then suggested she find as many possible ways of expressing this as she could. In such situations, I may offer other examples, such as, "For many people, life can continue to be pleasant and successful" or "There is no reason for your life to not continue to be pleasant."

The person might be ready to discuss an experience early in the fifteen minutes and may even feel her experience is complete. If this does not occur, at the end of the fifteen minutes the person is asked to describe or review her experience. Sometimes the fifteen-minute period provides more than enough time for the experience. If the client wishes to continue for more than the full fifteen minutes the drumming is continued.

The Feathered Serpent:
A Death of the Old and Birth of the New
Typically, a journey into the underworld of the unconscious mind examines the source of the person's problem and often reveals the healthy words that need to replace the dysfunctional words that the person has been unconsciously saying. What is found most often is some dysfunctional way a parent or significant other related to the person, usually some form of neglect, abuse, guilt trips, or overly high expectations and demands for perfection; or the parents' own emotional problems may have interfered with healthy ways of relating early in life. These are just a few possibilities, but while in trance the suggestion, "Let the wisdom of the adult self go back to help your younger self understand" often leads the person to realize that the burden the parent or significant other

placed on them was inappropriate or unfair. As we have just shown, the person can be led to a healthier way of relating with the suggestion, "Let the wisdom of your adult self go back and help your younger self find the right words to say what you need from your parents." These words of what is needed need to be stated in a positive way, not the negative words of what is not needed; a discussion in the therapy session can assist the client in adding to this list of needs; for example, "Dad, I need you to listen to me and be gentle with me," or "Mom, I need you to let me be a child and enjoy childhood things."

In introducing the Feathered Serpent the client is instructed to stand tall, with the backs of the hands resting on the hips and elbows out to each side of the body. I then ask the person what he thinks the posture expresses. With some prompting the client can be led to realize that it expresses a feeling of determination—the determination to let the dysfunctional part of the self die and a healthy part be born. With the preparation offered by the Lady of Cholula and Jivaro postures in previous sessions, the client has by now gone beyond the fear of change, or death, and is now ready to incorporate the needed change within his unconscious, a rebirth.

After practicing and thereby understanding the intent of the Feathered Serpent posture, the client is then instructed to first assume the Bear Spirit posture. After a few minutes of relaxation and ego strengthening like this, the drumming begins, the client and I both standing together in the Feathered Serpent posture. A one-sentence suggestion is offered: "Let what you need from your parents lead you to becoming the good parent in your relationships with others," or some variation on this that may fit better with the client's situation. At the conclusion of the fifteen minutes of drumming, the client reports the experience, an experience of the death of the dysfunctional way of thinking and a birth of a healthier way of thinking that gets implanted in his unconscious.

For the woman waiting for something bad to happen, while standing in this posture she repeatedly said to herself, "Bad things do not necessarily have to happen, and waiting for something bad to happen is a waste of time," and "For many people, life can continue to be pleasant and successful. There is no reason that my life should not continue to be pleasant," and any other similar thoughts that she added to the list.

When to Reveal?

At this point the decision to discuss the names and provenance of the postures depends on several factors, as described below.

The first cycle of using these four ecstatic postures sequentially—the Bear Spirit to provide relaxation and ego strength, the Lady of Cholula for divination to provide some direction and to answer questions, the Jivaro for journeying into the unconscious mind to find a solution and initiate the beginning of change, and the Feathered Serpent to provide a death-rebirth experience—sets the stage for offering the client a glimmer of hope that some changes in life are possible and even expected. The underworld posture may be repeated before the death-rebirth posture is attempted if it seems that the client is not ready or prepared for the rebirth. With this sequence of postures, a problematic part of the person dies, and what is reborn or retrieved is the innocence of the person's soul. This is the essence of soul retrieval.

This process or cycle of soul retrieval can be used again and again to bring about deeper and deeper changes that lead the person toward a greater level of maturity, until the problem that brought her to therapy is completely resolved. Until now, in living with the emotional or behavioral problem, the client has been stuck at a level of self-centeredness that prevents further growth. As the person begins to open up and relate to others in a more mature manner, displaying more empathy and concern for others, she moves into a higher level of awareness, a more mature developmental stage.

Fairly early on in therapy, possibly after this first cycle of experiences or perhaps after a second round of experiences, there will likely be a brief hiatus in the urgency of facing the problematic behavior as the client begins to integrate the changes and become part of a family and small world of friends and associates, people of like mind. While beginning to discover this stage of socialized consciousness, the person may reach a plateau. It is at this point that a new dimension or aspect of ecstatic therapy can be revealed to the client, in which the names and provenance of the postures are explained.

This is the point at which I share the story of Felicitas Goodman and her research into ecstatic trance and how she discovered the power of these postures. You can explain that Goodman searched through the literature and museum artifacts looking for what she thought were postures used by shamans or healers of various hunter-gatherer cultures. The client has already discovered the power of these postures, so hearing that they were used by these shamans or healers can be appreciated. Pictures of the artifacts are shared, and the names of the postures are given. I happen to have several artifacts in my office, two wood carvings of the San Blas Indians of Panama standing in the Bear Spirit posture and a museum reproduction of a Nordic image standing in the Feathered Serpent posture. I point these out to my clients. Revealing this kind of information makes further instructions in using the postures much easier. As well, in that these postures come from diverse cultures at different periods of time, it helps to open the person up to a whole new world of diversity beyond the self-centered problems being faced in therapy. The discovery of the world of diverse cultures is just one more step that can lead someone to a greater level of maturity, with the hope that one day he or she will become an elder, a person who can live equitably within a diverse world, working for the good of all.

SPIRIT GUIDES:
ALLIES IN THE PROCESS

Another dimension of ecstatic therapy is the use of spirit guides—in fact, spirit guides are evident in almost every ecstatic experience. I use the term *spirit guide* as frequently as possible to acclimate the client to this concept. For example, in reliving an experience from your younger years, your younger self can be called a spirit guide, and I frequently suggest that an ecstatic experience will lead you to or provide you with a spirit guide who can help you through this journey.

What is useful in discussions about spirit guides is to provide the client with images that reflect in some way some trait or behavior of the person. For example, from the case studies that follow in the next three chapters, one person "buried her head in the sand" to avoid something in life. After I used this image, she found an ostrich as a spirit guide in a trance experience. Another person was a rescuer, a person who had a need to be needed. I mentioned at one point in our conversation that she was the "seeing-eye dog." As a result, the seeing-eye dog came up in one of her experiences, and from it she found the strength to become the self-sufficient wolf. These spirit guides provided her with direction.

Simply mentioning stereotypical traits of animals can lead to useful spirit guides appearing in the ecstatic journeys—for example, the vulnerability of a lamb, the ferociousness of a lion, the phony cuteness of a poodle, the cunning of a fox, the working-together of a pack of wolves. All can become useful spirit guides in an ecstatic journey after they are referenced in conversation during the course of a therapy session. These guides can become important characters in the deeper unconscious stories or narratives that arise in ecstatic trance.

After the person has discovered the power of several spirit guides in leading them to new ways of thinking or experiencing themselves, there will come a time when explaining and teaching the person the power of calling the spirits of each direction fits in nicely in therapy. The spirits of the East are the spirits of the sunrise, of spring, and the birth of new life. The spirits of the South are the spirits of the warmth of the middle of the day, summer, and growth. The spirits of the West are the spirits of the sunset, of autumn, of the harvest, and of the productive years of life. The spirits of the North are the spirits of the nighttime, of winter, of hibernation, sleep, and death in preparation for a new birth in the spring. The spirits of the heavens are the spirits of the cosmos that placed Earth in the universe such that it sustains life, and the Sun and Moon determine the seasons, night and day, and the ocean tides. The spirits of our great Earth Mother are the spirits that sustain us, the spirits of everything of the Earth and the interdependency of all things of the Earth. Also, any one of the ecstatic postures can be talked to as if it is a spirit guide.

The appearance of spirit guides represent a progression in the evolution of a person's consciousness. They open him or her up to a whole new world, a world beyond one's self-centeredness. First, going beyond your self-centeredness in relating in a healthy way to people around you takes you into socialized consciousness. Then discovering the value or power of different cultures opens you up to cultural consciousness. And in discovering the power of animal spirit guides, you become open to the revelation that the Earth and all her beings are sacred. When an animal becomes your guide on the wisdom path, how can you continue to see yourself as superior to that animal? In this way, ecstatic trance work leads to a higher level of consciousness.

The Olmec Prince Posture:
Becoming Your Spirit Guide

Once the client has become familiar with the aforementioned four basic postures, I like to use the Olmec Prince, a metamorphosis or shapeshifting posture. In this posture you become your spirit guide, experiencing the guide from within, as that guide. This is useful in bringing the spirit guide alive within the person.

To begin, the client is instructed to sit cross-legged on the floor with a straight back, leaning forward such that he can place the knuckles of both hands side by side on the floor in front of him. For those who may find this posture uncomfortable, the use of pillows or yoga blocks may offer support. With frequent use, it did not take me long to find comfort in this posture. When asked what this posture expresses, it is generally pretty obvious that the knuckles on the floor represent the arms becoming forelegs. Even so, after some experience with this posture I have become a bird, a snake, and even a tree—all obviously without forelegs. As with the other postures, I take the same posture as the client during the fifteen minutes of drumming.

Using this posture brings the person farther along on the path toward spiritual consciousness. One central problem in our world at this time is our greedy attitude of seeking to profit from the Earth's resources, an attitude that is quickly and tragically leading to our own demise as well as the extinction of countless species and life forms. We modern humans tend to regard ourselves as some sort of superior life-form, especially to those things that we think of as being inanimate. When I am led to finding a spirit guide, whether flora, fauna, or a so-called inanimate thing like a river or a mountain, I have something—and often a lot—to learn from this spirit guide. With what I learn from the guide, how can I then consider myself better than the guide? In becoming the spirit guide I become one with the Earth and value it with profound gratitude. This is just the attitude of spiritual consciousness that is the ultimate aim of soul retrieval through ecstatic trance work.

3

Finding Fulfillment Within

A Case Study of
Panic Attacks and Dissociation

What about Coyote as survivor? The coyote that has extended its domain across the continent is an animal who is adaptable, who will try anything. If we truly want to be healers, we must be willing to use anything that works, regardless of our theoretical positions. Because if it works, it's good medicine.

LEWIS MEHL-MADRONA

Pam, age thirty-one, found that over the past year she had developed a severe case of agoraphobia accompanied by panic attacks. Three miles has become a magic number—whenever she ventured more than three miles from home she had a panic attack. At our first session we spent some time talking about possible triggers for the panic attacks, discussing her activities surrounding her panics, but nothing made sense to her. She only knew she had them whenever she left home, and that panics after three miles had become a surefire thing, a self-fulfilling prophecy. Her first panic had occurred at the shopping mall about four miles from home.

I wanted to offer Pam something to think about or do during our first session, and what made the most sense to me was to teach her a relaxation exercise that she could practice at home. I did not want her to use it yet in her travels because relaxation is a skill that has to be learned, and attempting it this early on might likely lead to failure. The relaxation exercise I recommended was the Bear Spirit posture, though I did not call it that initially. I simply demonstrated it to her, explaining that it was a relaxation and ego-strengthening exercise. I had her stand tall, with her hands resting on her abdomen. I asked her what she felt while standing in this posture, and she said that she could feel her abdomen rising and falling as she breathed, which was just what I wanted and expected her to feel. I suggested that she could feel a strengthening and healing energy entering her body with each breath, and as she exhaled she should let that energy flow throughout her body. I instructed her to stand in this way as I turned on a recording of some quiet but rapid drumming. Though some clients might question the use of drumming rather than some quiet new age music as used with hypnotic induction, I explain this by saying that there are different forms of trance, and I have found that this kind of mild stimulation to the nervous system is very effective in keeping the experience alive within the person and preventing the distraction of extraneous thoughts, which satisfied Pam.

As I stood in this same posture I told her I would be quiet much of the time but would occasionally offer some guidance in this relaxation technique. As she stood with her hands on her center of harmony and I observed her breathing, I suggested, "As you inhale, feel a sense of calmness enter you, and as you exhale, let that calmness flow throughout your body." After some silence, I added, "As you inhale, feel a healing energy enter you, and as you exhale, let that healing energy flow throughout your body." Then again, after some more silence, I said, "As you inhale, let the calming energy quiet your mind, and as you exhale, let that quietness flow through you."

I continued in this way, speaking once maybe every minute or so to the rhythm of her breathing for the five minutes of drumming. After this short session ended I gave her a CD of the drumming and asked her to practice this exercise as often as she could during the week, repeating to herself the same words that I had used or similar ones. I hoped she would practice daily. The recorded drumming provided a bridge connecting this, her first ecstatic trance session to her practice at home and would help induce the altered state of trance I wanted for her.

Normally, the induction ritual for ecstatic trance includes smudging to cleanse one's aura and calling the spirits of each direction. Those who come to me for psychotherapy for the first time, however, have certain expectations, and these parts of the ritual would seem very odd to them in this setting; thus, for a time they are omitted. Yet the necessary elements for ecstatic trance to occur were already present even in this first session: The therapy room is automatically experienced as a sacred space, especially after the element of client-therapist confidentiality is explained. Discussing what is expected from a trance experience fulfills the second requirement, that of reassuring the person that the experience is normal and pleasant. Though the hypnotic suggestions given during the drumming are not specifically part of what Felicitas Goodman taught, they increase the assurance that the person will go into a relatively deep trance that will help her quiet her mind; relatively soon, words become less necessary, and I no longer need to provide these kinds of cues. The rhythmic stimulation of the nervous system is accomplished by playing the CD of the drumming. And the Bear Spirit posture works quite well as a meditative technique to quiet the mind and prepare the person for the idea of using ecstatic postures later in the course of therapy. Thus, whereas with other forms of psychotherapy and hypnosis only the thinking mind is involved, the use of this and the other body postures involves the total person in the process of trance.

The following week Pam reported some success with the exercise I had taught her. She had practiced at home with the drumming CD I had given her and said she was able to feel more relaxed, calmer, and stronger. After repeating this relaxation exercise in the office, I suggested that this week she try driving her car a short distance from home, less than three miles, to a place where she could park and practice this exercise in privacy, standing next to her car with the window open so she could hear the recorded drumming from the car's CD player.

The following week she told me that she had driven to her girl-friend's house and parked in her driveway. Again, she practiced at home and found success in calming and quieting her mind. She had no panic attacks during this time.

The third week I assigned a bigger challenge: I told her she was to drive until she began to feel slightly anxious, at which point she should park her car and practice the exercise. This place may not be private enough to stand next to the car, so I suggested that she first practice the relaxation exercise that I had taught her at home while sitting tall, and then practice it sitting tall in the car at her house before she attempted to drive some distance from home.

I believed that something more than simple distance was triggering Pam's panics. I expected the problem was something she was saying to herself, some thought, most likely unconscious, something that we would, eventually, uncover. This beginning of therapy, which asked her to consciously and deliberately use an exercise that helped her relax, would set the stage for her to eventually take responsibility for overcoming her problem rather than just sit back and passively wait for a "cure."

Pam returned for her next session disappointed—she told me she'd had a panic attack when she went to visit a friend who lived nearby, less than two miles away, the friend whose driveway she had parked in to practice the first time. This panic attack was as bad as any she had experienced.

"When did the panic happen?"

"Just as I was parking the car near her place."

UNCOVERING THE REAL PROBLEM

"Okay, it's time to begin to go deeper to uncover what triggers your panic attacks. This time sit at the edge of your chair with your back straight and with your hands clasping your knee." This was, of course, the Lady of Cholula divination posture; however, as with the Bear Spirit that I had taught her earlier, I did not use that name in the session. "Take a few moments to feel what the posture expresses." After a few moments I asked her to describe what she felt.

"It feels like I am waiting for something, something important," Pam said. This exploration of the feeling expressed by the posture introduced her to why we use it.

I prompted, "Yes, the answer to your question as to what is causing your panic attacks. Okay, first, before we use this posture, I want you to stand with your hands resting on your abdomen, your center of harmony, and feel the calming and strengthening energy of each breath calming your body and mind. Take a few moments to focus on your breathing, and when you hear the drumming, sit straight on the edge of your chair with your hand clasping your knee and watch for the answer as to the question of what is causing your panics." As she assumed the Bear Spirit posture, I too stood with my hands on my center of harmony. After Pam stood there for about five minutes, I turned on the recorded drumming. We both sat down in the Lady of Cholula posture, and occasionally during the fifteen minutes of drumming I would use the words of suggestion, "Let this trance journey carry you to the source of your panic attacks," or some similar words speaking slowly, following the rate of her breathing. After the fifteen minutes of drumming ended, I asked her to tell me what she had experienced.

"What first came to mind was a dream I had a couple days ago," she said. "My daughter Tammy was out with her friend. While they were gone I got a telephone call from the police to come and pick her up. She was in trouble. I raced out of the house in a panic. Then I woke up in a panic."

While we'd been sitting in the posture I had felt this panic coming from her. I asked, "What did she do to get in trouble?"

"I don't know, smoking pot . . . I don't know. Maybe she shoplifted something."

"Okay, what part of you got into trouble or gets into trouble?"

"I hate to say this, but I shoplifted something a couple of months ago."

"Tell me about it."

"I was in Walmart. I went into a dressing room with something to try on, along with a package of panties. I took the panties out of the package and stuffed them into my purse. That way I didn't think the alarm would be set off when I left the store. I know some stores have something in the merchandise that will set off an alarm if you try to leave the store without paying for it. That was just before my panics started. Actually, I've shoplifted a few times. I know it's wrong, I could have paid for the panties, but I just did it pretty much without thinking. I don't know what made me do it."

I mentioned to her that "Tammy" in this dream was actually an important spirit guide. As the session came to an end I suggested that we return to this experience at the next session.

From my experience, bringing up the thoughts and feelings that occurred in trance at a previous session of therapy often takes the person right back into a very mild state of trance. So at the next session I reviewed what Pam had experienced in her previous session. I told her that this time we would try a different posture to go into the underworld of her unconscious mind, and that in that way she could delve deeper into her experiences of the previous week, of her dream and her experience at Walmart. Then I demonstrated the Jivaro Underworld posture (though I didn't call it that) while lying back in my recliner and had her practice the same posture while lying on the sofa in my office, the back of her left hand resting on her forehead.

It was apparent that this discussion of the posture and her previous week's experience was already leading her into a mild trance, but to deepen her relaxation we once again started out with the Bear Spirit, each of us standing with our hands on our center of harmony as we consciously followed our breath. After a few minutes of this I turned on the drumming CD; she reclined on the couch as I laid back in my recliner. Throughout the trance session, I occasionally offered the hypnotic suggestion of going back to her dream and even further back to when she first shoplifted. After fifteen minutes the drumming ended, she described her trance experience:

"I was in Walmart. I walked by the display of panties and stopped and found my style and size. I took them into the dressing room, took them out of the package, and put them in my purse. Then I went back to my dream of a phone call from the police."

"How did you feel while you were taking the panties?"

"I don't know. I really didn't feel anything. I don't even need more panties. I just took them without thinking."

"You weren't thinking, you just did it. You know it is wrong. You don't know why you did it. Stay with those thoughts. Go back to your dream. You get a phone call from the police. Be you in the dream."

I again turned on the drumming CD. She was still lying on the couch, and I too reclined back in my chair.

After a few minutes of lying there I asked, "How do you feel?"

"Scared."

"You don't feel angry?"

"No, just scared."

"Stay with your scared feeling. What part of you is scared?"

"I'm scared that I might get caught."

"You are scared for yourself, not your daughter."

"Yeah."

I could feel the anxiety and fear rising in her.

"Okay, now go back to when you went to your girlfriend's house and were scared, panicked actually, when you drove up to her house. Stay with that scared feeling. What are you scared of now?"

"I'm scared to go shopping with her. I might shoplift something. She told me once that she had shoplifted something. I just might do it with her."

"Think of another time you had a panic attack. What were you doing?"

"Driving to the mall."

"To go shopping?"

"Yeah."

"And another time?"

"Yeah."

"Okay, with all the wisdom and understanding of your adult self, help yourself understand. Stay with those thoughts. Stay with them for a few minutes, and when you're ready take several deep breaths and open your eyes."

AVOIDING FEELINGS

By now Pam was beginning to understand the source of her panic. She saw that by not thinking she was able to avoid taking responsibility for her actions. One goal of the next session, therefore, would be to bring her guilt, shame, and fear alive within her in order to end her tendency to dissociate, to separate herself from her consciousness, from the knowledge or understanding of why she shoplifts, knowledge and understanding that she has suppressed into her unconscious mind. For this we would again use the Jivaro posture. I told her that after our initial standing relaxation exercise where we hold our hands on the center of harmony and focus on our breathing, I would start the drumming CD and we would both lie down—she on the couch and I on my recliner. I then started the recorded drumming as we both reclined, and said just a few more words to give her some direction for her trance experience:

"Go back to your dream. Go back to sitting in the car next to your girlfriend's house. You are having a dream. Let's finish that dream. You get a telephone call from the police to come rescue your daughter. Take your time . . . When you get that phone call, lift the index finger of your right hand . . . Okay, feel the panic as you race out of the house and drive to the police station. There is a parking spot near the front door of the station. You pull up ahead of it and back in. Your heart is racing. You get out of the car and lock the door. You walk around the car and step up on the curb next to the meter. You open your purse to take out some change to put in the meter. You turn and walk toward the entrance of the police station. You take hold of the door handle and pull it open and go inside. Across the room is a counter; a police officer sits behind it. You walk up to him and identify yourself, showing him your driver's license. He tells you how the mall security guard called him after a store manager reported your daughter shoplifting. The officer gives you a paper to sign. He takes you back to a cell where your daughter is waiting. You look in through the bars, but you don't see your daughter, you see yourself. You feel the wind go out of you. Stand there and see yourself behind bars. It is you behind the bars." I then remained quiet for the rest of the fifteen minutes. At the end I asked her what had happened.

"All that I could think of was, 'What will my daughter think? What will her father, what will her stepmother think? What will everyone think? I would lose my job.'"

"What *will* they think?"

"That I'm bad. I'm a disappointment to her. Her father could try to take her from me. I could lose my job at the prison."

Pam had owned her feelings of fear, guilt, and shame for a full fifteen minutes.

I then reflected back to her what she had been feeling in "yes-set" statements, in order to maintain trance. "You are a bad example to your daughter. You are bad. Stay with and own those thoughts. Don't let them go. Shoplifting is wrong. You broke the law. You did something bad. You are bad. Hold on to these thoughts. Feel bad. Feel guilty. Feel ashamed. Take those feelings and thoughts with you. Now go back to Walmart. Again you are walking through the panties department. You stop and pick up a package of panties. Hold on to the thought *I am bad. I am a bad example for my daughter.* Feel the humiliation of letting everybody down, the fear of losing your daughter to her father, of losing your job as a guard at the prison. Let those feelings grow inside you. Let those feelings panic you. Put the package of panties back on the rack. Leave the store. Go back to your car and sit there; breathe. Feel proud of yourself."

Pam was led to own her experience rather than separating herself from it by placing it on her daughter. The ego-strengthening experience offered by the initial use of the Bear Spirit posture helped to give her the strength she needed to own the experience. Yet dissociation is a powerful defense. I expected that her pattern of dissociation would be a continuing issue that could interfere with her changes unless she faced the underlying reasons.

BACK TO BEGINNINGS

At the next therapy session I told Pam that I thought we were ready for her to go back to the beginning, back through time, to when she first felt the need to shoplift. To do this we used the same posture, beginning with five minutes of relaxation in the Bear Spirit posture and then, when the drumming began, we both reclined in the Jivaro posture to explore her unconscious drives. I occasionally and repeatedly offered the hypnotic language of, "As you go back through time, watch the days, months, years go by, carrying with you the thoughts and feelings of when you shoplift. As you go back through time you will soon become aware of an important incident that led you to shoplifting." After the fifteen minutes of drumming ended, I asked Pam to describe her experience in the present tense, as if it were happening now, so that the immediacy of her trance experience would continue, thus furthering her recall.

"I am young, in middle school. I am shopping with a girlfriend and her mother. Her mother is buying my friend her first bra. I feel bad; I want one too. A couple of days later I go back to the store by myself and take a bra that is just like my friend's, though it is too big for me. I don't want to bother my mother for getting me one, and I believe I need one. My mother was real sick at the time, on chemotherapy."

Though Pam could have felt guilty for her youthful transgression, I noted that she instead found two justifications for stealing the bra. I suggested, "You buried your head, your feelings, in the sand. I think it would be useful to find a spirit guide to help you." With those few words, I suggested that she again stand for a few minutes with her hands on her center of harmony to feel a healing strength flowing into her body, and we both got up and stood like this. Then after a bit I suggested that she sit down on the edge of her chair and clasp her knee in the Lady of Cholula posture. I turned on the drumming CD, and we both sat in the posture. After fifteen minutes of drumming ended, I asked her to describe her experience.

"I was in a dry and sandy place where I saw an ostrich with its head buried in the sand. I walked up behind it and kicked it in its backside. Its head popped up, and it looked bewildered. The light seemed so bright and confusing." She had taken my suggestion and was running with it; she was owning her feelings of bewilderment—bewilderment regarding her absence of guilty feelings.

"Your spirit guide, the ostrich, does not know what to think. She *should* feel guilty but doesn't feel especially guilty unless the anxious feeling is the feeling of guilt. Let your adult self go back and be with your younger self and help your younger self feel the feeling of guilt. Take your time. The feeling of guilt has not been readily available to you, but it is an important feeling of life. Imagine feeling guilty . . . let that feeling of guilt become real."

This was a minor breakthrough; Pam was able to relate to these words. The feeling of guilt was not strong and real to her—in fact, she couldn't even remember a time she had felt guilty, but she could feel a heavy or empty feeling in her chest, maybe a sign of the presence of guilt. That feeling could be much like the feeling of anxiety or panic— the very thing she had come to therapy to heal. That feeling of emptiness would have greater significance as our therapy progressed.

Pam came to therapy the following week with another dream, again, of her daughter:

"I saw Tammy stabbing and killing a woman. There was blood all over the wall. I saw what was going on but did not feel especially bad, though I questioned myself about my responsibility in the murder. I don't remember anything else but blood on the wall, and I thought I should feel more upset or guilty."

In her dream, Pam went to the most horrifying crime she could think of that should trigger feelings of guilt. Though in the dream she put the responsibility for the crime on her daughter, when I asked her to let herself become her daughter in this murder scene she couldn't or wouldn't. Her only thought was of all the women in the prison where she worked as a guard who had actually committed murder but who continued to put the blame on someone else and did not feel guilty or remorseful. Pam's defense mechanism of displacing her guilt onto someone else was very strong. Her tendency to dissociate allowed her to avoid painful feelings for much of her life. Whether it was in turning in a homework assignment late or breaking up with a high school boyfriend, she was very good at turning off her pain and getting on with life. In some situations it might have been helpful, in others not. Typically dissociation is a very difficult pattern to break, and she might likely never give it up totally. As therapy progressed we would try to find ways for her to more constructively deal with it while trying to solve her immediate problem of compulsive shoplifting.

Since Pam first mentioned shoplifting five weeks earlier, she had thought constantly about it. She had struggled to not shoplift and had only shoplifted once during this time, about two weeks ago. "The more I think about this problem, the worse it gets," she confessed. "I'm so worried that I'll get caught, but I can't seem to stop."

When I saw Pam again two weeks later, she said she hadn't shoplifted. It was now four weeks since the last time she had shoplifted. The last time we met I left her with the suggestion that she stay with her feelings of guilt and anxiety—the tightness in her chest and shortness of breath—to see what message these feelings might bring her. She had followed these instructions for a while but became exhausted by the feelings and slid back into her default pattern of pushing painful feelings out of her mind. She also had not gone shopping. Whereas these feelings had been coming out indirectly in her dreams of her daughter and in her agoraphobia, a fear that kept her away from the shopping mall, the dreams had also ended. The goal in therapy was to get Pam to consistently and directly face the problem of shoplifting and her anxiety, guilt, and agoraphobia, in order to overcome her defense mechanism of dissociation. That she had shoplifted only twice over the last few months, and not at all for the last four weeks, also diminished her feelings of fear, guilt, and obsessive thinking associated with shoplifting. But at least this emotional distancing from her problem now made it easier for her to examine it and talk about it.

THE TRIGGER

Pam was now able to describe her pattern of shoplifting—that when she was in some emotional struggle in her life as she had been five years earlier, when she went through a divorce, she had shoplifted more frequently. In between such struggles she would not shoplift at all. Since her divorce she had gone through two boyfriends. During the times she was being courted by these men she had shoplifted some. There was some anxiety in being courted, she admitted, but her shoplifting became much worse when the relationships came to an end. She had not shoplifted for six or eight months until about three months before she entered therapy, when once again she shoplifted. She had not had a boyfriend for nearly a year, and her shoplifting first started when her mother was being treated for cancer. So what was the stressor in her life now? One possibility was that she had been feeling lonely and anxious about not being in a relationship. Probably the best time in her life for not shoplifting had been the first few years of her nine-year marriage. Then, as the marriage deteriorated when she learned that her husband was having an affair, she started shoplifting again.

Pam actually found strength in her freedom to talk about her pattern of shoplifting, something she had never done before, and as a result she wasn't dissociating as much. It was easy to talk about it because it seemed to her like it was something in the past, or like somebody else's problem, and not something that involved her directly in the here and now. Talking relieved her anxiety about the problem. Since she was in therapy she hoped that the problem would simply disappear, and certainly four weeks was a good start, but only a beginning in this process of self-discovery.

I was concerned that Pam was becoming too comfortable with her life and that her complacency made her more vulnerable to her pattern of dissociating. Realizing that she did not shoplift when she was comfortable with life gave her another defense mechanism to avoid facing her problem and to rationalize it by blaming it on any stress she might be experiencing at the time, such as the loneliness of being between boyfriends. We hadn't used ecstatic trance for a couple of weeks in therapy, not since her ostrich experience. At this point I felt it was important to get to something deeper. I suggested that we needed to go into the underworld of her unconscious mind. I expected that this would take her back to her experiences with her mother. After the few minutes of standing with our hands on our center of harmony to quiet our minds, we both lay back in the Jivaro posture as the drumming started. After fifteen minutes she related the following:

"I have very little memory of my father. He left when I was in elementary school. My mother then raised me as a single parent. She worked, but we had very little money. She barely made enough for us to have a roof over our head and food on the table, even with help from my grandmother. One day she asked me to dust the living room, and I was dusting the shelf with the glass animals. She had a collection of small glass figurines of animals on a shelf in the living room that I liked looking at. I picked up the glass hen and dropped it, and it broke. I was scared and hid it from Mom. When she found it broken she knew that I was the only one around who could have broken it. But she didn't get mad; she just told me she wanted me to buy her a new one. I had a little birthday money and took it to the store and bought her the hen. It was only seventy-five cents—I remember giving the clerk a dollar and getting a quarter back. She was happy and smiled when I gave it to her."

"Did you feel guilty?" I asked.

"I don't know; I don't think so. I was scared that she would be mad, but she wasn't. I think I was just relieved that she had asked me to buy her another one."

Feeling guilty did not seem to be part of Pam's makeup, though feeling scared about the possibility of being caught was a very real emotion for her. The fear of being caught was what we had to work with in therapy, and that would have to be sufficient.

FACING HER PROBLEM

Then another issue came up that brought her compulsion to the forefront. One of the prisoners was found with a marijuana joint and accused Pam of giving it to her. Such complaints had to be investigated, and in the process of the investigation the corrections officer is often considered guilty until proven innocent. Such charges often leave the officer feeling helpless: "How can I prove I didn't give it to the inmate?" The evening after receiving this notice, Pam stopped at the mall and shoplifted some panties. This time Pam was horrified, which brought her fear alive. She was in a real state of despair. She couldn't dissociate this time. While in the process of stealing the panties she wasn't thinking, but immediately afterward, while driving away from the store, unable to dissociate, she felt real fear and felt like a failure. Whereas before she would panic when she thought about going shopping, now the panic happened immediately after she had stolen. When she got home, the phone rang and she panicked, thinking that she had been caught. When her daughter called out for her to answer the phone, she had difficulty lifting the receiver up, but the call was for her daughter. Every noise inside and outside of the house put Pam on edge, and she was a wreck.

Pam was gasping for air as she described this experience. I said, "You could be thankful that this happened because now you are more prepared to face your problem and not run away from it." This comment shocked Pam into regaining her composure, and we were able then to accomplish something in the session. In reality, Pam's panic *was* healthy. Upon hearing this story in therapy, I reassured her that this was a giant step in the right direction because she was not dissociating, and not dissociating took great strength—the strength necessary to be more honest with herself. The feeling of guilt was not yet there for her, just the fear of being found guilty and getting fired from her job. But at least she was feeling her feelings.

The fear Pam had experienced was such that she wanted to avoid the store for a while. I thought that for her to return to the scene of the crime would cause her to feel her guilt, and so I encouraged her to go back to the store and this time buy some panties: "Intentionally go into a store, pick out the panties, take them to the counter, and pay for them." The expense was not that great, so she said she would do it.

At the next session Pam related this very revealing insight she'd had after following my suggestion. "This is crazy, but when I held them, they did nothing for me. The words that came to mind were, *They weren't given to me.* Those were the exact words that came to mind. I've been thinking about it. Something is special about panties when they are given to you. It was special when my girlfriend's mother bought her the bra. It's crazy. I know the store didn't *give* them to me; I stole them."

"Your mother was too sick to take you out and buy you your first bra or buy you the panties you needed. You felt empty when she was unable to give you the loving intimacy and understanding a young girl needs from her mother as she matures."

With newfound resolve, during the next couple of weeks Pam did not shoplift despite her work anxieties. The day came when she went before the fact-finding hearing that was investigating the allegations against her. She denied the charge and stated that she didn't use or have access to marijuana. The hearing was just to collect information, so no conclusion was reached, but Pam still felt very rattled by the hearing and resentful that the prison officials didn't trust her word over an inmate's. That evening she shoplifted. Pam came to her next session chagrined. When she was emotionally down she had shoplifted, putting her job in jeopardy if she had been caught. If she lost her job she would have no one to blame but herself.

BECOMING THE GOOD MOTHER

Picking up where we had left off with our trance work, I suggested that we return to the underworld to explore her unconscious further, to find other examples of her feelings of emptiness, examples that we could use to effect change through trance. After standing for several minutes with our hands at our center of harmony to quiet the mind and gain the ego strength necessary for the exploration we were about to embark on, I started the drumming recording. We both assumed the Jivaro posture. I began, "Go into the underworld as you think about your mother. During your teen years she was suffering from cancer and was unable to give you what you needed. Your girlfriend's mother gave your friend her first bra. Your mother was unable to take you shopping. You understood why, yet you still felt very empty, just as you feel empty now. There is no one who can help you at work. When your mother was sick you went out and stole your own underwear. You didn't have the money to buy it, so you took care of yourself this way. Somehow that took away the pain of your emptiness. Last week you learned that buying underwear didn't bring you any satisfaction because it was not 'given' to you, so you felt empty."

At the end of the fifteen minutes of drumming Pam related the following:

"I just got back from shopping with my girlfriend and her mother. I ran into the house to tell my mother about what we had done. I heard the toilet flush and saw my mother coming out of the bathroom and flop into her chair. I knew she had been in the bathroom throwing up because of the chemotherapy. She sat in her chair looking awful and breathing heavy. I told her about Janey getting her bra, but Mom just sat there breathing hard. I went upstairs to my bedroom and cried."

I responded, "You are crying. Stay with those feelings. Listen to the feelings, the hurt, the emptiness. Think about the words that describe those feelings. Breathe deeply and slowly. With each breath watch those feelings within you spread throughout your body. Don't forget those feelings. Again, take those feelings with you and go back further in time." She was still lying on the couch in a trance, so I turned the drumming recording back on.

After five minutes, Pam spoke up: "I'm in the kitchen. I'm telling Mom that we won. I was playing softball on the junior high softball team. She says, 'That's nice,' but she is not really listening to me."

I suggested, "Have your adult self go back and be with your junior high self. Your adult self knows your younger self better than anyone else. With all the wisdom and understanding of your adult self, help your junior high self understand. Tell me what you are feeling, what you are thinking."

"I ask Mom to come to the game, but she says she can't. I think she's watching the soaps. She always watches the soaps. It would be good for her to get out of the house. She's been that way ever since she found out that Dad was having an affair. She doesn't have time for me. She works at night and is always tired."

"Let your adult self help your junior high self find the best words to describe how you feel. Your adult self knows the feelings of your younger self better than anyone else. Tell me how your younger self feels."

"Empty . . . hurt."

"Stay with those feelings. Listen to your words: *She doesn't have time for me. She's always tired.* You feel empty and hurt. Tell me what other feelings you are feeling."

"Just empty and hurt."

"Do you feel any anger?"

"Maybe . . . a little."

"Okay. You feel empty and hurt, maybe even a little angry. Again, go back further in time." I turned the drumming on again.

Five minutes into the trance Pam broke in: "I'm coming into the house. Mom is on Dad's case again, yelling at him about something. I want to tell Mom something, but I forget what it is. I just go upstairs, throw myself on the bed, and put my hands over my ears. I think I fall asleep. I don't remember what happens."

"Again, let your adult self help your younger self understand."

"Yeah, I am angry at Mom. Hurt, angry, and empty."

"Bring all three times together, your mother being sick because of chemotherapy, your mother being preoccupied because your father is having an affair, and your mother being on your dad's case. Feel the feelings of emptiness, anger, and hurt. Again, let your adult self be with your younger self, and with all the wisdom and understanding of your adult self, help your younger self find the best words to say what you need from your mother."

"I need her to listen to me."

"Think of more ways to say that, of more things that you need from her, and in saying them, say them *to her*—use the word *Mom*: 'Mom, I need you to listen to me.'"

"Mom, I need you to come to my softball games."

"Okay, take some time this next week to think of more of what you needed from your mother. We will come back to this same place next week. Spend a few moments breathing, watching your breath. Breathe slowly and deeply, and gradually become aware of your body, of the world around you. Then open your eyes slowly."

The following week I said that it was time to try something different in therapy.

"Stand tall with your feet planted about shoulder width apart, knees slightly bent," I instructed. "Place the back of your hands on your hips, like this." This, of course, was the Featrhered Serpent posture, though I didn't call it that as I demonstrated it to her. "Stand that way for a few moments to experience how that posture feels. What does it express?"

"My mom would stand like that when she was trying to get me to do something. She was angry."

"Maybe, but put yourself in front of some task. Imagine that you are standing in front of some project you are working on or trying to accomplish. What are your feelings now?"

"Oh . . . determination. I am determined to do it, to finish it."

"That's what it feels like to me too. It gives me the energy of determination, of facing something somewhat daunting that I am ready to face, possibly something in my life that needs to change. But first, before we use this posture, let's briefly review what you experienced last week. Bring together coming home to your mother after your friend got her first bra, after winning a softball game, and when your mother was on your father's case. Feel the feelings of hurt, anger, and emptiness from these experiences. Your adult self knows your younger self better than anyone else. Let your adult self help you find the words to describe what you need."

With this preliminary suggestion, I continued: "Okay, stand for a few minutes with your hands on your center of harmony to quiet your mind and feel a strength growing within you." I stood with her in this posture. Then as the drumming recording started, I joined her in standing in the Feathered Serpent. After the fifteen minutes of drumming ended, I asked Pam to tell me about what she had experienced in trance.

She started off by offering another statement of what she needed from her mother. "Mom, I need you to turn off the soaps and stop being so angry at the world." Pam was now clearly expressing her anger.

I suggested, "Can you say it in positive terms, of what she *can* do? When you say what you are not going to do, it does not tell you what you can or should do."

It was obvious that Pam had been thinking about this. "That's hard . . . 'Mom, I need you to do something with your life, to take charge of your life. Mom, I need you to think positive.' My aunt used to tell me how self-centered she was. 'Mom, I need you to think about me, think about other people's feelings.'"

"Good. What you need can be said in so many ways. Speaking while in trance carries the words deeper into your unconscious mind. I want you to continue thinking about what you need over the next few weeks, but for now let's take this to the next step. I want you to say these same things, but address them to yourself. Your mom is within you. When you become what you need from your mom, you begin to heal those painful feelings of hurt, emptiness, and anger. 'I need to listen to others. I can become a better listener.' Think about what you need from your mom, and become what it is you need."

I again turned on the drumming, and Pam put her hands on her hips with a sense of determination, while I joined her in the posture.

"I need to pay attention to others. I need to pay attention to Tammy. I need to go to Tammy's school plays—but I already do that. I need to get a life. I need to think about other people's feelings."

"You do pay attention to Tammy, at least more than your mother did to you. You do have more of a life than your mother's. You do get out with your friends, and you do date. But you can always do more, and when you are with your friends or on a date, you can always think more about how the other person feels. Working in a prison does strange things to a person. You may have some sympathy for some of the inmates, but you cannot let yourself get too emotionally involved with them. You also may find yourself feeling disgust for some inmates. You cannot let your relationship with an inmate become a healthy relationship like it can be with your daughter, friends, or a man you are dating. As you develop healthy and fulfilling relationships with others, you won't feel as empty yourself. These next few weeks try to be aware of how you want to be different from the way your mother was, and practice being that way."

BONDING

By being a better listener and by being present for her daughter and her friends, Pam began to experiment with bonding. Though Pam had never experienced a healthy, bonded relationship with her mother and thus had no understanding of how such a relationship would feel, this assignment gave her an opportunity to experience bonding to some degree. She might not understand the feeling, and it might frighten her at times—issues that we would face in therapy. Nevertheless, Pam was beginning to move from self-absorption to learning how to empathize with others and respond to their needs. This was a developmental shift.

At her next session, Pam mentioned that the following week was going to be Tammy's fifteenth birthday and she wanted to do something special for her but didn't know what. She had all kinds of ideas, from a surprise birthday party, inviting Tammy's friends, to having Tammy invite her friends for some other activity, but she didn't know where to start in inviting Tammy's friends. She knew some of their names but didn't know how close they were with Tammy or who they all were.

I suggested that if she knew one of Tammy's close friends she could ask that person to help in making the list of friends. Pam thought that something was going on between Tammy and her best friend and that this girl might not be the best choice. I asked if Tammy had a boyfriend, and again Pam thought that she was between boyfriends—she had a potential new one, but the relationship was too new. Then I asked

Pam what was most important to Tammy, and Pam said that it was her friends. Pam really didn't seem to know Tammy that well, something I had noticed earlier in therapy. I suggested that doing something with Tammy, just the two of them, might be more important to her daughter, as well as be a chance for her to really pay attention to Tammy and to learn more about what is going on with her now. Teenage girls always like to go shopping. "Take her shopping and go out to lunch and get her talking about her friends and boyfriend. Let it be a mother-daughter birthday, a time to learn the meaning of bonding." Shopping was a trigger for Pam and made her nervous, but the purpose was to bond with Tammy. "A shopping trip with Tammy may feel different enough such that shoplifting might not be an issue. Maybe buying Tammy underwear would be important, something your mother didn't do with you."

Pam usually gave Tammy money to go shopping with her friends. They had gone shopping together, but only when Tammy wanted something specific, or else Tammy told her mother what she wanted and Pam would get it for her. Shopping trips were never really fun events, going out just for the sake of shopping. "Maybe going to a totally new place, the outlet stores in Lancaster, would be fun. The two-hour drive would be time together to talk. It's important for you to do a lot of listening and very little talking. Maybe buying underwear for yourself while buying it for Tammy would make it special."

I thought that Pam might feel anxious about spending that much time alone with her daughter, but she thought it was a great idea. I expected that a teenager might really open up with her mother when they were alone together and she was the center of attention, and that conversation between mother and daughter would be no problem.

Pam and Tammy did go to Lancaster and had a great time. Pam said that she felt like a teenager again. "Spent too much money, but it was fun. We bought underwear for Tammy, and I got some of the same. It's not what I usually wear so it feels different. The trip did feel good. It was something I've never done before with her."

"People change and do things differently. Maybe that could be a change in your life, a new life of closeness with your daughter, of bonding with her. Wearing different things would reflect this change within yourself of discovering the meaning of bonding, bonding that fills your feeling of emptiness. She is no longer a young child, and she may be a little young to be your friend, but maybe it's time you start becoming more of a friend than a mother."

It was time to reinforce what was learned the week before in stating what Pam needed to do to become the good mother to Tammy, in this way bringing the feelings of bonding more alive within her. "Let's return to the posture of determination, with the backs of your hands on your hips, with the determination of being the sensitive mother in listening to your daughter."

After the initial ritual for induction and standing for fifteen minutes in the Feathered Serpent posture, Pam recounted her experience while in trance:

"I first saw the ostrich shaking her head in bewilderment, feeling all alone, feeling confused by the bright light, but especially feeling empty. Then another ostrich strutted up and they put their short wings around each other. It felt good to not be all alone with my head buried in the sand. The ostrich coming back surprised me, especially the feeling of emptiness, of being alone in the desert and with its head buried."

"There was another ostrich to relate to, to hug you," I said. "You were not alone after all. You felt all alone with your mother, but you can be the good mother with Tammy. You have someone in your life you are learning to bond with. The ostriches are valuable spirit guides for you. There are other ostriches in the desert."

I decided that now that Pam was comfortable with all four postures and had made some progress with them, it was time to reveal the source of the postures.

THE STORY OF THE POSTURES

"Pam, the ostrich is an important spirit guide for you. Besides burying their heads in the sand, ostriches are not always alone and can embrace each other. We will explore more about spirit guides, but first I want to tell you about Felicitas Goodman's research on ecstatic trance. She was an anthropologist. This is the fourth posture we have used. This posture, with the back of your hands on your hips, she called the Feathered Serpent. She searched through museums and books on the ancient and contemporary art of primitive cultures around the world and found what she thought were the postures used by their healers, their medicine men. She found and experimented with many of the postures, approximately fifty, and found that specific postures had specific effects on the ecstatic trance experience. The Feathered Serpent is found in many cultures around the world. I have pictures of this posture from over a dozen different cultures, but the first image of the Feathered Serpent she found was Mayan. This posture typically produces a death-rebirth experience—the death of a problem or something dysfunctional and the birth of something functional, a healthier way of being. For you, it is becoming a healthier mother in relating to Tammy.

"The first posture we used was with your hands resting on your abdomen, your center of harmony. Felicitas Goodman discovered that it brings healing and strengthening energy into your body, an energy that also can quiet your mind. Though again this posture is found among most of the cultures of the world, the first image of it that she found was from the northwest coast of North America. It was of a figure being hugged by a bear. She called this posture the Bear Spirit. The second posture, where you sit on the edge of your chair clasping your knees in a certain way, is the Lady of Cholula posture, which was found in Cholula, Mexico. This posture is used to find answers to specific questions and to find direction in one's life. The third posture we used, where you lie on your back with your left wrist resting on your forehead, was from the Jivaro Indians of South America and is for journeying into the underworld. We call it the Jivaro Underworld posture. I have found these four postures especially powerful and useful in giving direction in therapy, though I do occasionally use some of the other postures.

"Using this sequence of four postures is sometimes referred to as *soul retrieval*. It means bringing back some part of the self that was lost long ago." I had some pictures of these postures to show her as I described them. Pam seemed interested in and attentive to this story of the postures. She was ready to look beyond herself and her own pain and open herself to the world beyond her, in this case to the people of different cultures and how they lived.

HUGGING

Having told Pam about the origin of the postures, I now felt it would be useful and timely to add another posture to our repertoire, the Olmec Prince, a metamorphosis or shape-shifting posture that facilitates becoming and learning from a spirit guide or spirit guides. I had her sit on the floor with crossed legs, the knuckles of her hands resting on the floor in front of her. She was quick to recognize that in this position her arms were like the front legs of an animal. I told her, though, that in this posture I often became other than a four-legged animal. I would often become a bird and suggested that it could bring her to becoming the hugging ostrich, the ostrich with its head buried in the sand, which represented her. The ostrich who hugged her was now a new part of herself, a new side of her that was beginning to develop. It would be most valuable if she would become the hugging ostrich, to experience that new side of herself in greater depth.

After the initial ritual of quieting the mind and finding ego strength with the Bear Spirit posture, I started the drumming as we both sat on the floor with the knuckles of our hands on the floor before us. At the conclusion of the fifteen minutes of drumming, Pam reported her experience:

"I did become the hugging ostrich, and I felt good reaching out to the other ostrich and hugging it. After having its head buried in the sand for so long it needed a hug to face the world. After we got back from our shopping trip to Lancaster, Tammy had a big hug for me, and it felt so good. We have been hugging a lot ever since. I don't remember many hugs since she became a teenager, and my mother and I never hugged. The ostrich told me that it was something that I needed and I think Tammy needs too."

Pam said that after their shopping trip Tammy seemed to want to talk with her mother more often. She would run into the house when Pam was home, eager to tell her about her day. Pam had become a good listener with her friends, and now she was relating to Tammy more as a friend. Tammy was a good girl and ran with a good crowd. Pam had little to complain about, until one evening when Tammy came home late. Her new boyfriend had his driver's license, and for the first time coming and going didn't depend on Pam or the parents of Tammy's friends. Pam didn't know what to say to Tammy, afraid that some of the good feelings between them would be lost if she confronted her. Pam needed to step up to the plate as Tammy's mother, yet it was evident that she wasn't comfortable in that role.

LIKE MOTHER, LIKE DAUGHTER

Pam telephoned me a week before her next scheduled session saying she needed to come in as soon as possible. I saw her the next morning. She arrived red-eyed, looking as if she hadn't slept for days. "Tammy's pregnant," she gasped. "She wasn't telling me everything that was going on when she was with her boyfriend. What can we do? She has to finish school! She has to go to college! I so badly wanted to go to college, but I had Tammy when I was sixteen. Tammy will be sixteen."

Pam's mind was racing, as it had been the whole night before she came in for her session. Her words spilled out. "After Mom died, I lived with Gram until I was fourteen. I didn't see much of my father after he left when I was in elementary school. But after Mom died I needed him, and he started coming around. When I was fourteen I moved in with him. Dad thought then that I could take care of myself when I was home alone, so he got a place for us. I was a good student. Tammy is a good student. I wanted to major in criminal justice and become a police officer, but then I got pregnant.

"Near the end of the pregnancy I moved back in with Gram since they thought I needed someone near me all the time, and I lived with her until I finished high school. After she was born she took care of

Tammy. I wanted to go to college and major in criminal justice, but no way could we afford it. I took a job in a factory and then a year later got the job at the prison, the next best thing to police work. Tammy was six and in school when we got our own place. I was making good money. It was then that Tammy's father moved in with us, and we eventually got married, but that only lasted four years. He now lives in Tennessee with his new wife. She has taken some interest in Tammy. They are Facebook friends, though they have never met face-to-face.

"Back then I would drop Tammy off at Gram's on my way to work, and I got home by two-thirty, before she got home from school. Gram would get her off to school. I want Tammy to go to college . . ." She started beating her fists on her knees. "I took a couple of night classes at the college, but it was too much. Tammy would stay with Dad on those nights. But Tammy needed me. I wanted her to have a mother. I wanted to give her my time after work."

"What is Tammy thinking?"

"I don't think she has any idea how hard it will be, but she hasn't told her boyfriend yet. She's afraid to tell him. He just wants to have fun, and I . . . we don't think he is ready to settle down. She has always talked about going to college. She still wants to go. I think she thinks that she can take the baby to classes with her. She just doesn't know." Again she started pounding on her knees.

I responded, "There's one big difference: You had your gram and your father. Tammy has her mother who really understands, something you didn't have. Even though you haven't known how to be close to Tammy until recently, you can feel close now because your life is repeating itself. Just the way you are feeling it now, you will be doing this together. It won't be easy. I'm sure you will beat on yourself at times. Somehow it helps you to feel the pain." Pam's newfound innocence in the closeness she was feeling with her daughter was dead. She again felt all alone and empty in the grief she felt about her daughter's pregnancy. But this time her grief was alive. She was really feeling her feelings like never before.

She continued to pound on her legs, to feel the pain of her grief. "But how can we do it? How can Tammy go to college?"

"You look back to when you had Tammy, and it's so scary. You're pounding on yourself in grief and in frustration, the frustration of 'how are we going to do it?' That word *we* is so powerful. You are in this with her. She is the most important person in your life."

"I need to stop by the mall on my way home from here. Tammy needs something for school. I'm glad she's still thinking about school, but I can feel myself . . . I know I'm going to want to shoplift."

NEEDING A MOM

"You know, you want your mom with you in this . . . You know you want your mom with you in this . . . You need the understanding support you have to offer Tammy for yourself, from your own inner mother. You need your mother to give you support, the way it would feel if someone were giving *you* panties, giving *you* emotional support. Let's stand in the Feathered Serpent posture. Feel the strength in that posture. Let's have a conversation with your mother. You can tell her all of what you have told me and more. Have you visited the cemetery recently? You might want to go there to talk to her, or you might want to talk to her while holding the glass hen or one of the other glass animals, maybe the glass giraffe or the glass horse."

After the initial ritual for relaxation and ego strength, I turned on the recorded drumming, and we stood in the Feathered Serpent posture. After a few minutes, well before the drumming ended, Pam spoke up:

"When I broke the glass hen, Mom was not angry, though I was afraid of what she would do. I was relieved that she asked me to buy her a new one. I remember being afraid after that to pick up the animals. I did think she was mad when she would put her hands on her hips and give me her stern look."

"After you buy her the new one, you're in the car driving home with your mother. What is going on?"

"Nothing. We're not talking. We're quiet. I don't remember talking to Mom unless I needed something."

"Sort of like it was before between you and Tammy?"

"Uh-huh."

"It's hard to talk with your mom. What do the glass animals mean to your mom? You seemed to enjoy looking at them."

"I don't know. I used to enjoy arranging them in a parade or like in a zoo, or maybe in the jungle. I didn't put the lion next to the pig because I knew he would eat it. I never thought about it, but some were farm animals and some were wild animals."

"Did your mom have them arranged in a certain way?"

"I don't know . . . I don't think so. She let me arrange them the way I wanted."

"It sounds like she had them there for you."

"Maybe, but she was protective of them."

"Was there an ostrich among them?"

"I don't remember one . . . I don't think so."

I was trying to find a sensitive side of Pam's mother, but everything came up distant. "Take a few moments to feel the warmth and closeness you have with Tammy . . . Feel the hug of the ostrich. Now take that feeling with you back through time, to a time when you were with your mom." I was then quiet. She was still standing in the Feathered Serpent posture, and the drumming continued.

After a few moments, Pam said, "This isn't working. I don't think I ever felt close to Mom. I know she loved me because she took care of me, but we never talked, never shared feelings like Tammy does with me."

"You and your mom seemed to never talk; there wasn't that closeness that you feel with Tammy. You felt alone in the desert."

Pam still felt empty. However, there was hope, because she was able to feel close to Tammy, and she had learned that closeness somewhere. Maybe I was trying too hard. Maybe I should have been following the energy of Pam, but I hoped I could find some instance of closeness between Pam and her mother. Weeks ago Pam had revealed that her problems with shoplifting represented her desire for closeness with her mother. Earlier in therapy I had assumed that this need developed out of the death of her mother at a time when she especially needed her. It was now evident to me that this lack of closeness between them went back even further, even before the onset of her mother's cancer.

AVOIDING GUILT

A week later, at our next therapy session, I suggested using the Jivaro Underworld posture. As we laid in the posture I suggested, "Imagine telling your mother about Tammy's pregnancy. What do you think she might have said?"

Pam quickly responded, "'You make your bed, you lie in it.' That was something Mom said a lot. I remember when I was young I didn't understand what it meant, but I knew I had done something wrong . . . I was thinking last night that Tammy should feel guilty about getting pregnant. I think I should feel guilty for failing to teach Tammy how not to get pregnant, but I don't feel especially guilty. I feel more guilty about not feeling guilty."

Though Pam was feeling fear, frustration, and grief, guilt was still inaccessible for her. Neither did she feel any great remorse when she herself had gotten pregnant when she was still in school, or when she shoplifted, and she didn't feel any remorse on Tammy's behalf. As the drumming continued, I mimicked, "'I should have. I should have.' See where that takes you."

After a while, Pam spoke up. "I should have said 'no' to sex. I should have gone to college."

"You should have said 'no' to sex. Hold that thought." The drumming continued, and I suggested, "Go back further."

Soon Pam's breathing became more shallow and rapid. "I should have been there when Mom died."

"Go on."

"I found her dead in the bathroom. Blood was everywhere. She had been throwing up blood. I should have been there sooner. I should've done something. I thought of putting a washcloth in her mouth to stop the blood. Now I know that wouldn't have helped her."

"You should've done something."

"Yeah, I should've done something. But then I guess I just stopped and wouldn't let myself think that."

"You wouldn't let yourself think, *I should have done something.* You wouldn't let yourself think, *I should have said no to sex.* You don't let yourself think, *I should have taught Tammy how not to get pregnant.* You have learned to not think, *I should have . . .* You have learned to not feel guilty. Now you question yourself that maybe you *should* feel guilty, or at least feel guilty for not feeling guilty."

The following week we saw that her dreams were giving continued direction to Pam.

"I dreamed that my mother, Tammy's grandmother whom she never met, was telling Tammy that it's okay to get pregnant. I remember having the same dream when I was pregnant, of my mother telling me it was okay to get pregnant. I remember waking up the next morning feeling rested for the first time in weeks. Mom was supportive."

"And you didn't have to feel guilty," I countered. Pam had found a way to protect herself from feeling guilty. For her it didn't take much to avoid feeling guilty, yet she couldn't escape the responsibility of becoming a mother.

PLANNING FOR TAMMY'S FUTURE

The time we spent trying to bring Pam to be in touch with her guilt was short. Something else was on her mind. Now she was preoccupied with her plans to get Tammy through college. She admitted that it was going to be a strain both emotionally and financially, but she was high on the process of planning. The problem that I foresaw was that she, and not Tammy, was taking the initiative and responsibility for planning ahead. Pam's trap was to allow Tammy take advantage of her willingness to rescue her. Though it may not always be healthy, I have seen many empty-nest grandmothers take over raising their grandchildren in order to refill the nest. For Pam, the situation presented an opportunity to mend the weak bond between her and her daughter, but so far she was being action-oriented in providing material support rather than relating with emotional support. She was being a "human doing" rather than a "human being."

The responsibility and strain of her offering Tammy the support she needed to give birth and get through college finally hit Pam a couple of weeks later. The strain was first seen in Pam's dreams:

"I had two dreams. In the first I am leaving the prison at the end of my shift. There are usually two or three locked doors I go through using my key to get off the unit and out of the building, but in the dream I'm unlocking door after door and checking to see that each door locks behind me. I don't know how many. I woke up exhausted. I don't think I ever got out. The second dream was the same kind—I'm driving home and the road goes on forever. It's really a short distance for me to get home from work, but the signs keep saying another five miles or another mile. It's bizarre. I don't know if the blocks were just real long or what, I don't think I was really lost. I think I knew where I was going, but the distance seemed hundreds of miles rather than just three miles. I never got there before I woke up."

"Dreams can create such distortions," I replied. "What is really three miles can seem like three hundred miles. In both dreams you are just not getting to where you want to be. I bet in the second dream you also woke up tired. It seems like it's taking so long to get Tammy through her process. She hasn't even had her baby yet and is still in high school. Could that be what you are dreaming about?"

It might have seemed easy for Pam to dissociate from her feelings of guilt and get on with life; after all, she had had so much practice over the years. But this dissociation was not healthy. By giving herself—her time and her money—to Tammy, Pam was in her own way showing love to her daughter, so her compulsion to shoplift panties in order to feel loved and pampered was no longer necessary. Giving everything to her daughter and soon-to-be grandchild was only a temporary solution, however. Eventually, when Tammy became independent of Pam, the empty nest would feel extremely empty, and Pam would again need to pamper herself.

RECURRING STRUGGLES

Because of the strain and frustration of her situation—strain likely to last the next six or more years—recurring struggles between mother and daughter would be very likely, times when one would push the other away. These struggles would likely leave Pam feeling empty and stimulate her urge to shoplift. These struggles might also be revealed in dreams, such as the one that Pam offered a month or two later. In the interim I had offered little more than supportive listening to the details of the activities of Pam and Tammy. Pam was driven to share with me what they were doing to prepare for the birth that would come a couple of weeks before Tammy was to return for her last year in high school.

Pam expressed that she wanted to continue therapy, mainly for the emotional support she needed. It was September, and Tammy was back in her final year of high school soon after her baby, a girl whom they had nicknamed Sunshine, had been born. Pam was working second shift, so there was only about an hour between the time she'd have to leave for work and the time that Tammy got home from school where she was able to babysit Sunshine. Pam's dream occurred the night after someone at work had commented to her that maybe she was doing too much for her daughter, and that Tammy needed to learn to be responsible for herself and her new baby. This was because Pam had been complaining about being tired at work. She was really bothered by this suggestion. Though Tammy would get up once or twice during the night to nurse the baby when she cried, Pam was up several times at night to give Tammy a chance to get some needed sleep; she was having her first test of her senior year and wanted to do well.

"I dreamed that the roof just lifted up off the house. I woke up screaming. Just a week or two ago I saw pictures of the hurricane that came through Florida and lifted the roofs off houses. I think my screaming woke the baby, because she was crying too."

"What a nightmare! What in your life is so frightening?" I asked. I probably didn't have to ask that question; the answer seemed pretty obvious. But the question revealed several different answers or levels of answers: Pam's fear of Tammy's test the next day; her own fear of being too tired the next day at work; the fear that someone might again tell her she was doing too much for Tammy. But in talking about her fears, deeper fears emerged: the fear that she could fail in supporting Tammy; the fear that she might lose her job and not have the income to support Tammy; the fear that she didn't have the emotional strength to support three people. Pam was feeling very vulnerable. She needed someone to pamper her rather than to be critical of her as her friend at work had been. Pam admitted that when she woke up from the dream she went to her dresser drawer and found a new pair of panties that she held to her cheek. She was able to fall back to sleep holding the panties.

I thought that it was important for Pam to understand the agitation she felt when the person at work told her that maybe she was doing too much for Tammy, that Tammy needed to learn responsibility. So we stood in the Bear Spirit posture for a few minutes to quiet the mind, and then we sat in the Lady of Cholula posture while she asked a question about why that comment had made her feel so agitated. I turned on the drumming recording. Soon Pam interrupted the drumming to say, "I can't be like my mother and tell her to lie in her own bed. I need to take care of Tammy. She needs to go to college."

Pam's problem with shoplifting seemed like something in the distant past. She had been very involved with her new granddaughter and getting Tammy through her senior year in high school. She was feeling fulfilled in caring and doing for her daughter and granddaughter, showing them her love. She had no need to shoplift, to pamper herself this way, now that she had a granddaughter to pamper. Her attachment to her granddaughter filled the emptiness she had long felt because of her lack of attachment to her own mother. Her problem had been solved by doing. She was finding fulfillment in functioning in her role as a mother and grandmother, in her closeness with her immediate family. Yet there would be times of acute stress, when what she was doing was threatened or something went wrong, and she would feel overwhelmed. At these times there would be no one available to pamper Pam, and at those times she would likely revert back to thoughts of shoplifting. The original problem had not been solved, just pushed under the rug for the time being.

THE GOLDEN RETRIEVER

Pam appreciated having me to talk to and having my emotional support. No specific issues had surfaced that warranted the use of ecstatic trance in our last few sessions, yet I was well aware that ecstatic trance provides an avenue for personal growth and can be used for purposes other than seeking resolution for certain problems. We had last used it to help Pam understand why she felt so agitated when her coworker commented that maybe she was doing too much for Tammy. Now was a good time to take these thoughts and feelings into the underworld of her unconscious mind. After standing in the Bear Spirit to quiet her mind, I had Pam lie back on the couch in the Jivaro Underworld posture and started drumming, suggesting that she might like to find a spirit guide to help her with everything that was going on in her life.

After the fifteen minutes of drumming ended, Pam told me about her trance experience:

"I first thought of something I could cuddle, but I have the baby, Sunshine. I then thought I needed something reliable and strong, and a golden retriever came to mind. I have a friend with a golden retriever that is very gentle and protective of her children and is always right there. I was visiting my friend, and the dog came up in a very gentle way and nuzzled Sunshine. I cannot afford a dog to take care of and another mouth to feed, but it felt very comfortable to sit holding Sunshine with one hand on the retriever scratching its neck."

"You have found another powerful spirit guide, the golden retriever." I like to focus especially on spirit guides other than human spirit guides because it begins to move the person in the direction of spiritual creativity, of becoming one with our great Earth Mother, which is an expansion of consciousness and a recognition of our interconnectedness.

Despite all the new stressors in Pam's life, she was able to relax and feel the pleasure of having the baby to cuddle. She admitted that even when the baby was fussy, she was easily soothed with a warm cuddle. For once, Pam had a life, a fulfilling life caring for Tammy and Sunshine. Tammy had been breastfeeding, something that Pam wished she could have done with Tammy. Though they were both tired all the time, the baby had really brought the two of them together.

Some stress occurred a few weeks later when Tammy developed a breast infection. It began with a high fever that sent her to bed and caused her to miss a couple of days of school. Pam had to take family sick leave, and she knew the prison would give her grief. Pam actually enjoyed the days off, but when she returned to work she received a notice from the personnel department stating that her leave was unauthorized and that if she did it again she'd receive a one- or two-day suspension. Pam couldn't tell Tammy about this because she didn't want her daughter to feel like it was her fault. Pam realized she had no one who understood and no one she could call on to help out if this were to occur again. On her way home from work she briefly flirted with the idea of shoplifting—she felt she deserved to do something for herself—but the pressure to get home to see how Tammy and Sunshine were doing prevented her from acting on her urge.

As the session continued I suggested, "You were wise to not tell Tammy about this reprimand, because it would have made her feel guilty. You are becoming quite sensitive to the feeling of guilt, but there are ways of talking that do not impose guilt on someone. You're afraid to tell Tammy of your concerns and the things she needs to hear to become a good parent herself, afraid because you don't want her to feel guilty. What is something you'd like to tell her? Your golden retriever spirit guide taught you a gentle, nuzzling strength. Maybe your golden retriever can lead you to an answer."

CALLING THE SPIRITS

I continued, explaining to her how the postures that we use were used by the ancient healers who felt the power of the spirits all around them and found spirit guides among them. "As they went into trance they would call the spirits of each direction to learn the wisdom of these spirits. Let me call the spirits as I believe they called the spirits." So as we stood with our hands on our center of harmony, feeling the calming, healing energy entering our bodies, I summoned the spirits. "Spirits of the East, of the sunrise, of the beginning of life, bring us your wisdom and join us." As I called the spirits of each direction I offered them a pinch of cornmeal. Facing the South, I said, "Spirits of the South, of the summer and the warmth of midday, spirits of growth, of growth of our children and our gardens, we honor you. Bring us your wisdom, and join us." Then, facing West, "Spirits of the West, of the sunset and autumn, of the harvest of our gardens and the productive years of our life, we honor you. Bring us your wisdom, and join us." And facing North: "Spirits of the North, of winter and nighttime, of hibernation, dormancy, and sleep, bring us your wisdom, and join us." And then, looking up: "Spirits of the heavens that placed Earth where it can sustain life, with the Sun that brings us night and day and the four seasons, and the moon that brings us the ocean tides, we honor you. Bring us your wisdom and join us." And finally, "Spirits of Mother Earth who sustain us and all life, we honor you, bring us your wisdom, and join us." Last, I added, "The spirit of your cuddly and strong golden retriever, we honor you, bring us your wisdom, and join us."

After this induction ritual of calling the spirits and the mind-quieting experience with the Bear Spirit posture, I began the drumming recording as we sat on the floor with our legs crossed, resting the knuckles of our hands on the floor in front of us, in the Olmec Prince posture. At the end of the fifteen minutes of drumming, Pam reported: "I did become the retriever and watched Sunshine for a few minutes before I went over to her and nuzzled her with my nose. She grabbed my fur and pulled on it. That actually felt good, and I lay down next to her and she pressed her head into my side. I was so warm and comfortable. She soon fell asleep on me. I could see Tammy sitting nearby, smiling at us. Cuddling and hugging feel so good, something I now realize I have really missed."

"This next week just let yourself be the hugging ostrich, but especially be the cuddling retriever."

At the next session Pam brought in another concern. She felt that sometimes Tammy didn't understand what it meant to be a good mother—specifically, that babies need special care and are not ready to be adults. Tammy had been trying to get Sunshine to eat the same food she liked. With this comment I suggested that we see what the Feathered Serpent would have to suggest.

After the initial ritual, which included calling the spirits from each direction, we stood in the Feathered Serpent posture as I started the drumming. At the end of fifteen minutes Pam reported, "She sometimes tries to give Sunshine a bite of the things she is eating when she's not ready to eat that kind of food, like a little piece of sausage off the pizza. Though I told Tammy in a serious way that she needed to think more about how tiny Sunshine is and what she is ready for, I felt cuddly and gentle in telling her with the dog at my side. I was able to hug Tammy, and we laughed together. I felt the golden retriever was at my side."

It was evident to me that Pam was able to take charge of Tammy and Sunshine and do everything for them, and she was doing this in a gentle and sensitive manner. Tammy appreciated it on one level, appreciated being taken care of, but there may come a time when she might resent it.

At this point I was seeing Pam about once a month. She was doing well in most regards, but she still wanted to hang on to me for support and understanding in the long haul. Several months later, after the New Year, she came in for a session especially shaken. Tammy had received a phone call that worried her.

TAMMY'S BOYFRIEND

"When Tammy became pregnant she didn't tell her boyfriend. She just withdrew from him, and he didn't pursue her. He had phoned her a few times at first, and each time she was busy with homework or something. After she put him off a few times, he stopped calling. Though he was out of school, they were in the same circle of friends, and he started dating another girl in the same circle. He had to know she had been pregnant, but he obviously wanted nothing to do with it, which was fine with us. But why did he call now? Does he want to be part of his daughter's life? That would just complicate everything."

I suggested that it could help—"one more person for support."

"But he's unreliable. He's young and wouldn't be consistent."

"Maybe he's grown up. You had a father. Didn't Tammy have a father for her early years?"

"Not really. He just moved in for convenience. We eventually got married, but he was very irresponsible, was never there. Now his wife takes more interest in Tammy than he does. She's a Facebook friend of Tammy's."

"What happened with the phone call with the old boyfriend?"

"They talked for just a few minutes about a mutual friend who had moved out of the area, and he wanted her phone number. He didn't ask about the baby. Tammy said she had something she had to do, and then they hung up."

"That sounds innocent enough."

"He could've gotten the number from someone else."

Our conversation went on to other things—how the baby and Tammy were doing. Tammy was over her breast infection, and both were doing well. When the session ended, Pam wanted to make an appointment for the following week. She had had a feeling that something else might happen.

She was right. During one evening, Scott, Tammy's ex-boyfriend, popped in. It was just like old times, yet he appeared a bit nervous. It was obvious that he wanted to see his daughter. She was asleep, but Tammy took him in to see her anyway. He looked very uncomfortable and didn't know what to say or do. He looked at the child for a couple of minutes and then said that he had to get going. That was it. Pam didn't think he would be back, at least for some time. At this, Pam seemed to relax a bit. "Tammy didn't seem to have any trouble with it. She didn't say more than two words to him but just took him into the bedroom, and they both just stood there. I think Tammy wanted him to see the baby, but I think she doesn't think he'll be back either. Not a lot said."

Pam made an appointment for a month later. At that time she told me that Sunshine had been fussy and had developed a diaper rash, but that it was clearing up. Tammy was doing fine in school, though always tired, and nothing serious had beset Pam at work. The struggle to get through the next few years would continue. Again my role as therapist was that of being a supportive listener to their activities. Pam was coping with their activities in a relatively strong manner.

FURTHER REALIZATIONS

The ecstatic postures provide powerful experiences even when they are used without a specific issue in mind. This seemed to be one of those times for Pam, a time when things were going well. When she arrived for her session I suggested that we use the Jivaro Underworld posture to see where it might take her. After calling the spirits of each direction and finding internal strength and quietness with the Bear Spirit posture, I started the drumming recording as we lay back in the Jivaro posture.

After fifteen minutes of drumming, Pam related the following:

"At work I was walking through the cell block looking in each cell, checking on the inmates, when one threw a cup of urine through the bars. Most of it missed me. The inmates can be so disgusting. Several have babies that the foster parents might bring for a visit. I sometimes feel a little sorry for the mothers, but the baby is much better off in the foster home. The mothers are mostly incompetent as parents. Sometimes an inmate wants to talk, and I listen, but they're just trying to get me to feel sorry for them. Being in prison seems so hopeless. The inmates are learning nothing, and their lives are going nowhere. They can't be helped, at least in prison. They know if they behave they will get more privileges. Most of them know what it means to behave, and when they get out they will behave to get along while still doing what they want when others are not looking. I'm getting tired of such a meaningless job; it feels so hopeless." The job, though, was important to her to get Tammy through college. Stating these feelings of being dissatisfied with her job that came from this journey into her unconscious set the stage for the next few sessions.

Sunshine was now eight months old and getting into things, but Pam saw to it that she got plenty of love. Pam was now working third shift, the eleven to seven shift, so she was at home with the baby during the day. She still wasn't getting enough sleep, but she was getting by. At work, mandatory overtime was sometimes a problem, when her shift ran over and she had to work into the next shift, the morning shift. But Pam had found a Mennonite family that was willing to help out in an emergency. Mennonite families were a big help in fostering the babies born to inmates and bringing the babies to the prison for regular visits with their mothers. They were kind and gentle, good surrogate parents. Pam had arranged with one such family she had gotten to know to fill in for her in case of an emergency.

Such a situation arose when Pam had to work mandatory overtime and Tammy had to go to school. The school year was coming to an end. Pam knew by 7 a.m. that she was going to have to work into the next shift, and Tammy's first class started at 9, so Tammy had a little time to get the baby over to Lizzie, the Mennonite woman who was caring for Sunshine, and still get to school. But on this one occasion Tammy had a final exam scheduled at 8 a.m. and no one in Lizzie's family answered the phone. As it turned out, the family was at the hospital because Lizzie's mother had had a heart attack.

The prison administration was known for being very unreasonable, believing that work was the employee's top priority. Pam was ready to walk off the job, but she knew she could be fired and couldn't let that happen. The only option was for Tammy to take the baby with her to the final. Maybe her teacher would be more understanding.

Pam had no way of knowing what had happened with the baby while she was at work, stressed out because she couldn't reach Tammy by phone. Just like some people are driven to drink, Pam was driven to shoplift on her way home, and that is exactly what she did. Just holding a pair of panties was her fix, but she was so agitated that she aroused suspicion and was stopped as she exited the store. The security guard didn't know what to do when Pam broke down sobbing. He let her pay for the panties and didn't press charges. Pam was incredibly embarrassed. She hadn't shoplifted for about three years. Upon returning home she immediately called me for an appointment.

Pam was so embarrassed after this that she couldn't even imagine shoplifting again, but she had said that before. However, this was the first time she had been caught, and with this event she hit rock bottom. Though I forget whether it was she or I who first used the phrase that Pam "needed to be pampered," she was quick to identify with it. She knew that her dysfunctional way of caring for herself, of pampering herself, was to shoplift panties.

This was the perfect opportunity to use the Feathered Serpent posture. It was my hope that this death-rebirth posture would bring about the death of her dysfunctional way of caring for herself and the birth of a healthy way of pampering herself. After standing in the Bear Spirit posture to gather the necessary ego strength to embark on this journey, I picked up my drum and began rapidly beating.

After a few minutes, Tammy interrupted, though I kept on drumming, but more softly.

"In pampering myself, what comes to me is something I have always wanted to do, but my pregnancy with Tammy prevented me from doing it. I wanted to go to college, and at the time I wanted to major in criminal justice. Working at the prison didn't take a college degree and was the closest thing I could do in the field of criminal justice. I still don't think I can go to college, at least until Tammy graduates, but with everything that is going on now to get Tammy through, once she graduates it seems like that might be an easy goal." This realization brought a smile to her face. Her interest in going to college was renewed.

When Pam got home she had a chance to talk to Tammy. She found out that one of Tammy's girlfriends at school had been more than happy to take care of Sunshine while Tammy was taking the exam. Pam admitted that learning how easily Tammy had solved her problem actually made her feel somewhat anxious.

"You have felt quite fulfilled and satisfied in caring for Tammy and Sunshine. Discovering that Tammy easily found a solution to her problem takes you back to feeling unneeded and empty, but it also brings you closer to being able to pamper yourself by going to college. It is also time for you to feel proud of Tammy's ingenuity in taking care of herself. It's important for you to let Tammy know you are proud of her." Pam understood this, but the lifelong feeling of emptiness was still alive in her, and what fulfillment she had begun to experience was threatened. Then something else happened to further stimulate this perceived threat.

The following week Pam went to a department store with Tammy and Sunshine. Pam had seen a blouse she liked, and Tammy insisted on buying it for her. Pam so hated her prison guard uniform that she had always tried to dress stylishly when away from work, but over this last year she hadn't bought anything new for herself. She thought she couldn't afford new clothes and didn't really need them because off-duty her time was filled with caring for Tammy and the baby. On this occasion, however, Tammy wanted to pamper her mother. Pam knew that Tammy had no money of her own, that all the money she had had come from gifts from the baby shower, her birthday, Christmas, and money Pam herself had given her. Yet Tammy bought the blouse for her mother. Pam's response when Tammy gave it to her was, "Oh no! I can't take that. I want you to take it back." But Tammy insisted.

Pam finally took the blouse but felt very guilty. Her guilt was understandable this time, and it raised the question of what it means to be pampered.

"You can't deal with Tammy pampering you."

"I'm more concerned about her spending the money."

"But still, it was something Tammy really wanted to do for you. You have been doing so much for her. You hurt her feelings by not showing your pleasure and appreciation."

Realizing that Tammy's feelings had been hurt put Pam in a double bind. She felt guilty for accepting the blouse and for being pampered by Tammy. She also felt guilty for hurting Tammy's feelings by initially refusing the gift. I suggested, "Let's take those conflicted feelings you have into the underworld of your unconscious mind using the Jivaro posture. Maybe you will find a spirit guide who has something to teach you."

At the end of the fifteen minutes of drumming, Pam related the following:

"What came to me is 'Damned if I do, damned if I don't.' I recalled a high school girlfriend. She wanted me to smoke marijuana with her, and I didn't want to. I knew it was wrong, but I didn't want to be the prude and have her judge me. But I had a good excuse: I was going to college and majoring in criminal justice, and smoking pot would have interfered with that goal. I told her that I thought it should be legalized but that I couldn't smoke it now, and she accepted my excuse."

"What does that suggest to you that you could tell Tammy?"

"Oh, that is just what I was getting to. I could tell her that I appreciate her thoughtfulness and thank her, but that she shouldn't buy me anything else and should save her money for Sunshine and college. I did wear the blouse, though, and she was happy to see me wearing it."

"You found your spirit guide in your high school girlfriend who had shown you that you do have tactful ways to not hurt the feelings of others."

Pam returned to the next session more confused than ever. She told me she'd come home from work one evening to find a note from Tammy saying that she and Sunshine were staying overnight with a friend, Janet, the girlfriend who had cared for Sunshine during Tammy's exam. It seemed that Janet had become attached to Sunshine and had invited Tammy and her daughter to spend the night.

Pam said, "I don't know what to think. I felt very anxious and didn't sleep well that night. When Tammy got home she said that she really enjoyed the evening with this new friend. I feel like I lost something. I hate to use the word *jealous,* but I feel jealous. I feel confused. I shouldn't feel jealous."

"You shouldn't feel jealous. There's that guilt word again, *shouldn't.* Is there something wrong with feeling jealous?"

"I should be happy for Tammy and Sunshine."

"Can't you be both? What is jealousy anyway? They left you alone, abandoned you for the evening. You felt lonely, a look into the future when Tammy and Sunshine do leave you. By facing your feeling of jealousy, you begin to learn something about yourself, about life. Feeling guilty about feeling jealous only pushes it away and prevents you from learning that something, whatever it is.

FINDING HEALTHY FULFILLMENT

"Let's again use the Feathered Serpent posture." We stood with our hands on our center of harmony while I called the spirits of each direction. Then as I stood and started the recording of drumming, Pam placed the backs of her wrists on her hips as I did the same.

When the drumming ended, Pam said, "I had a thought the other day, but here it felt so much more real. I had a vision of being a student at the college, and I was walking across campus when I saw Tammy and Sunshine walking toward me, and then I saw Janet, her girlfriend, with Sunshine walking toward me. In both visions, Sunshine reached out to me and wanted me to hold her, and Tammy had a big hug for me. We were both students, and seeing each other at school was so much fun."

"Your nest may never truly be empty; with those hugs, your ostrich is around. Though Tammy and Sunshine will someday, maybe sooner than later, not be so dependent upon you, there will still be hugs, and you will find fulfillment in going to college."

At her next session, Pam told me that Tammy was thinking of moving in with Janet and living closer to campus. But the previous week's experience in therapy had been a stepping stone in providing Pam with a new way of reacting to this kind of news. She realized how unrealistic it would be for Tammy to start having to pay rent, and Pam wondered what her daughter would do with Sunshine if both Pam and Janet had classes at the same time. Tammy couldn't expect Janet to always be there to care for Sunshine, even though Janet seemed game to try. Pam said she was so shocked by the whole idea that she didn't know what to say to Tammy, so she had said nothing.

"I think it was the best thing you could have done, to say nothing," I told her. "Expressing your anxiety by saying something to try to stop her could have pushed Tammy to find reasons why her plan would work. By being quiet, you gave Tammy the chance to face the thought more openly and come to her own conclusion, the one you hoped for. It is so easy to say things to protect yourself, comments that often work against you. It's important to find the quietness within you to face your feelings. Again, feelings are opportunities to learn about yourself and find your power over the feeling. You are finding a new strength in yourself in facing all that is happening in your life.

"Now is the time to begin preparing for the empty nest. Now is the time to begin your search for that something that defines you, that fulfills you in a healthy way. Your search for your authentic self is a most important model for Tammy and Sunshine for eventually finding themselves. Your experience during our last session of going to college was a good start. It's an exciting thought to pursue. It's where you might find yourself."

Pam had made significant progress—from filling her emotional void by shoplifting, to filling it by nurturing her daughter and grand-daughter. Now was the time to begin searching for some lasting satisfaction, something that couldn't be taken away from her when Tammy would eventually leave the nest. There was one thing Pam could do that I suggested to her: The local college had a great career-planning program, and this program was offered to the community. She already knew about the program from Tammy, and with my encouragement she was ready to go. The battery of aptitude tests could give her some direction for what to major in.

About a month later Pam came to therapy with the results of her research. "I'm going to major in social work so that I can help teenagers," she reported triumphantly. The tests had suggested that her primary interest was in helping people. "The career counselor told me that a person interested in criminal justice is more interested in controlling people, and she didn't think I was a controlling person. That made sense when I thought about my relationship with Tammy. I think I've done a pretty good job with her, but I don't think I control her. I think I would be good at helping troubled teens, especially pregnant girls. I also thought about nursing; that's a possibility too. The college has both programs."

I could feel Pam's high energy. She was chomping at the bit to start, and the only thing seemingly holding her back was her need to care for Tammy and Sunshine. Pam realized that if she started college the following year, it would be Tammy's last year of her program, Pam's last chance to meet her daughter and granddaughter as she walked across campus. The community college program that Pam would be starting was a two-year program. My thought was that if Tammy and Sunshine did move out and were more independent, that Pam could maybe start the degree program at the college while still working. She would have more time by not having to babysit the hours she was not working. Her lack of money and her need to have Tammy and Sunshine stay at home were complicating her decision. So this was not the right time for me to make such a suggestion.

Instead, I said, "With this new strength you are finding within, let's again use the Feathered Serpent posture to see where this energy can take you." After calling the spirits of each direction and standing in the Bear Spirit posture to quiet the mind, I started drumming as Pam stood with the backs of her hands resting on her hips. When the drumming ended, she related this:

"I heard a deep growling sound coming from the drum. I felt it building up, building up inside of me. I wanted to throw my head back and roar like a lion or Tarzan. I felt such energy and strength building inside of me."

"I like your new lion and Tarzan spirit guides. They can help you a lot in all the changes that are happening in your life."

At our next session, I was glad for the groundwork laid in this session. Tammy had come home from school with the thought of finding a job near campus to earn money to pay for babysitting or day care while she and Janet were in class. She was also considering what other expenses she would have—rent, food, diapers, tuition, books—as well as calculating what kind of help she could expect from her mother. Pam needed this new roaring ego strength to handle this situation. I offered her one thought: "Tammy really trusts your strength in dealing with this situation."

"Oh! I don't think she has any idea how this frightens me. She thinks it would be easier on me if they were not so dependent on me."

"What did you have to say?"

"Just that we need to think about it. I was getting ready to go to work."

"That kind of thinking is very healthy for Tammy in facing her eventual independence. The best thing you can do is to sit down with her and look at the numbers. Make a list of the expenses if she were in an apartment on her own and the expenses of living at home; look at the differences, brainstorm all the factors. There are likely many factors that neither of you have considered. Tammy is of an age that it's natural for her to want to explore her independence. The issue you have to face for your personal growth is finding fulfillment in light of facing an empty nest."

Pam needed to keep the roaring lion alive inside of her, so I suggested that we use the Olmec Prince posture. After the initial ritual and sitting on the floor for the fifteen minutes of drumming, Pam reported: "I was stalking through the jungle, and there was a lot going on around me, a large snake sliding from a tree branch, monkeys screeching, loud birds, a branch crashing to the ground. The jungle was so alive, but I felt like the king of it all and would throw my head back and roar. I did that several times when something loud would happen near me. I felt that I could be louder than anything else. I felt like I was ready for anything." Her idea of pursuing a college degree in social work had made her feel as though she was on top of the world.

Pam was on a journey over which she had little control other than to take it one day at a time with a sense of curiosity, wonder, and openness, and she was finding a new, healthy strength to do so. She was no longer the self-involved woman who had first come to see me for her shoplifting compulsion and had found great comfort in a wider world of kinship, an expanded family. She had come to appreciate other cultures of the world as a result of knowing about and using the ecstatic postures. Majoring in social work in college, which she planned to start in the fall, would bring her into contact with all kinds of people and would thus move her into an even wider world, a cultural conscious-ness. Working in a prison where she needed to separate herself from the prisoners and to be their controller had trapped her; becoming the lion that roared was a sign she was ready to accept the challenge of evolving consciously.

Summer was approaching, and Tammy was close to finishing her first year of college. Sunshine was nearly two years old. Tammy had been promised a summer job as a waitress at a hotel restaurant near campus and was counting on getting good tips. She was still living with her mother and was still thinking and talking about moving in with Janet but had made no commitments yet. For one thing, the apartment they were considering was a one-bedroom, and Tammy and the baby would have to sleep in the living room. They had figured that Tammy would sleep on the couch, and that would leave enough room to set up Sunshine's crib.

It was Janet who made the move to change the situation. Her lease was up at the end of July. Her next-door neighbors were graduating, and their apartment had two bedrooms. Janet told Tammy that she was going to move into the apartment next door, which was larger and also had its own washer and dryer, though it was about a hundred dollars a month more than the smaller apartment. Tammy knew that Janet couldn't afford the increase in rent and was making the move with the expectation that Tammy and Sunshine would join her in the apart-ment. Janet thought the arrangement was perfect. She expected Tammy to pay only two hundred dollars in rent, which was very cheap for the area, and that would make it workable.

Pam told me that Tammy was excited about the possibility. "She is sure that with her job she can handle the rent and find day care for Sunshine. Sunshine will be old enough next spring that she should be around other kids. The college has a day-care center right on campus as part of their early childhood development program. She is count-ing on putting Sunshine in that program, but it won't start until the fall. She can sometimes go over and be with Sunshine between classes. So she'll be staying at home until August, when she and Janet move into the apartment. She wants to find a babysitter, and I can watch Sunshine when the babysitter is not available. Since I'm back to working the eleven to seven shift, I can care for Sunshine in the evenings when Tammy works."

I was pleasantly surprised by Pam's enthusiasm. The lion inside her was still alive and well. She had changed her thinking a lot over the last couple of months and seemed ready for an emptier nest. She was still somewhat concerned about money, however.

"I've agreed to pay Tammy's tuition and pay for her books," she said. "I may be able to scrape together another hundred dollars a month for her, but it will be tight what with my tuition and books next fall. I think I will take only a couple of courses at first to see how everything goes, and that way I can see Sunshine too. I think if I take evening classes my overtime won't interfere much, and I could use the extra money. I was thinking the other day how tired I used to be before Sunshine was born. Work and overtime wore me out. Now I get less sleep, but somehow I have more energy."

"You're not as troubled and depressed," I replied. "You are doing what you really want to be doing, and that gives you energy. That's a positive sign that you've made the right decisions."

Pam was excited about taking college classes toward a degree in social work and knew that working in this field would bring her a new sense of fulfillment that she had never experienced thus far in her life, except for the last couple of years in her newfound closeness to her daughter and granddaughter. After so many years of feeling empty, she could now go on with her life with a sense of satisfaction. Pam wanted to see me again in a month, but after nearly four years of therapy we could see its end coming in the near future.

Her initial panic attacks and problems with shoplifting had ended months prior. Having found new and healthier ways of fulfilling her feelings of emptiness, first in discovering a new closeness to her daughter, and now by looking forward to being a social worker, her limited world had expanded. Her ostrich, golden retriever, and lion spirit guides had allowed her to experience and value life beyond the human species.

She was entering a world of greater freedom in relating to others in a broad range of cultures. As a mentoring social worker within a diverse population she had the potential to become an elder to others, providing fulfillment in her life that could not be taken from her. I told her about the ecstatic trance group I offer that meets about once a month, but with all of the pressures on her at the moment, I did not expect her to be ready to take on another responsibility.

Through the course of her journey in ecstatic trance therapy, Pam had been able to overcome some troubling behavior that had not only caused her panic attacks but had prevented her from maturing into the woman she was capable of being. Using the ecstatic postures, Pam was able to gain insight and heal the source of her own pain, and in the process develop a greater sensitivity and sense of connection with those around her.

4

Transforming Anger to Transform Relationships

A Case Study of Control Issues and Insecurity

I had only to be faithful, and willing to stir things up a little, like Coyote.

LEWIS MEHL-MADRONA

Edward was sent to therapy by his employer because of his explosive temper. This was not the first time that his anger had caused him problems, but it was the first time his employer used the company's employee assistance program with the hope of resolving Edward's problem.

Edward, forty-seven, worked as an off-loader for when his company's product came off a particular machine. One day the product was turned in a way that made it a little more difficult for Edward to grab hold of it. He took it personally, believing the man who had loaded the machine was out to make his life miserable. Edward switched off the machine, stomped to the other end of the shop, and with clenched fists challenged the loader to meet him outside the fence. Edward was totally irrational. His feelings of paranoia and alienation were only

97

intensified by his employer's recommendation that Edward go to therapy. Being sent to therapy by his employer caused Edward to blame and resent his employer, so the possibility for any changes in therapy had already been undermined. As we shall see, it would take a more drastic experience of being fired before Edward would begin to take responsibility for his anger.

At his first session, after hearing his story I realized that in this situation there was one thing I had to offer, something that could be useful in future therapy situations and could be used throughout his life, and that was learning how to relax. He could take this skill with him and maybe use it in some life situations. He was not ready to otherwise dig deeply into his anger problem. The relaxation exercise I like to use also adds the element of healing and ego strengthening: the Bear Spirit posture, which I use in combination with the language of hypnosis. When initiating ecstatic trance with the Bear Spirit posture alone, the client's experience may seem empty and seem less effective. The hypnotic language of relaxation, however, deepens the experience, and in later sessions the hypnotic language can be eliminated.

I said, "Edward, I would like to first teach you a relaxation exercise that you can use in tense situations, but you need to practice it when you are feeling generally relaxed. It's a skill that once learned can be useful and healthy for anyone. I think it's a good beginning in these therapy sessions. I would like to have you stand tall and place your hands on your abdomen." I stood with him to demonstrate the posture. "As you breathe, air enters your lungs, pushes down on your diaphragm, and in turn pushes out your abdomen, the place I call the center of harmony. Feel your hands rising and falling with each breath, and as you inhale you breathe in a sense of calmness, and as you exhale let that calmness flow throughout your body."

I then turned on a recording of drumming, playing it quietly in the background as I stood in the posture and continued talking. "Let the drumming distract you from the many thoughts that go through your head. As you inhale feel the energy of relaxation flowing into your body. As you exhale, let this energy flow throughout your body." While following his breathing, after a minute or so I added, "Let the feeling of strength flow to your center of harmony, and let strength flow throughout your body as you exhale . . . Feel a sense of healing flow deep within you, and then let the healing strength flow throughout your body . . . Let this quiet relaxation flow through your head, quieting your thoughts." I continued in this vein, slowing down my speech as I observed his rate of breathing slowing down. This continued for the five minutes of drumming.

At the end of the session I gave him a recording of the drumming we'd used and suggested that he practice this relaxation during the week, daily if possible. The gift of the recording created a bridge between the experience of relaxation in the therapy session and the practice session at home, and it would become a trigger for going into a trance.

Edward made a commitment to remain cool at work. This commitment required willpower, but it takes imagination or an imaginal experience, as in ecstatic trance, to change a belief at the unconscious level, as willpower is usually not sufficient. Yet whether from denial or out of just being angry at the world, he blamed everyone else for his anger. Rather than accepting that he had a problem, Edward believed he had the right to attack those he felt were harassing him. Because of this blaming attitude I determined that he was not quite ready for therapy, but the employee assistance program had required him to go to at least three therapy sessions.

At the next session, I listened to Edward's report of the previous week. He did keep his cool at work, but he had practiced the relaxation exercise only twice during the week, claiming that he could not find the time to use it every day. I suggested, "When someone else gives you a hard time and takes advantage of you, it angers you. You can't let them take advantage of you. What was it like for you when you were in school? Would you explode when other kids harassed you?" I continued in this vein, without giving him time to respond to my questions, leading him into trance by using the yes-set. "Kids are quick to harass those who react in anger. Let's try another trance experience."

I demonstrated the Lady of Cholula posture and had him do what

I was doing, sitting straight at the edge of my chair with my left hand cupping my left knee and my right hand resting on my right thigh. I asked him what it felt like to sit that way.

After a few moments, he said, "I feel very alert."

"Alert in anticipation?" I prompted.

"Uh-huh, like I'm waiting for something to happen."

"Good, like waiting for the return of memories of what happened to you as a kid while in school. Let's both sit this way for a little while, but before we do let's go back to the relaxation exercise that we used last week to quiet your mind."

I had him stand tall with his hand on his center of harmony. Then I turned on the recorded drumming for five minutes as I stood with him in the same posture. While standing there I offered, "With each breath, inhale a sense of calmness, and as you exhale let that calmness flow up and down throughout your body. When your breath reaches your head, let it quiet your mind." At the end of the five minutes I put on a different drumming recording that lasted fifteen minutes and had Edward sit at the edge of his chair in the Lady of Cholula posture, as I too sat in the posture. I started out, "Let the drumming take you back to your school years, at a time when you were harassed by other kids . . ."

After fifteen minutes when the drumming ended, I asked Edward about his experience.

"I was in my first year of high school. After school I went to the bike racks to get my bicycle. A couple of the school bullies were there, and one pushed me, telling me he was going to take my bike. I remember I was glad I hadn't unlocked it yet. I looked around to see if I could see a teacher, and he shoved me again. I thought about running. I couldn't take on the two of them, but he grabbed my arm. I swung around and got him in the face. He let go, but the other kid kicked me in the back of my legs and I fell down. He jumped on me, but I put my knee up, and he got it in the balls. He fell on me and knocked my head on the pavement. I don't remember much after that. I felt dizzy and sick to my stomach. I think I somehow rolled over and started hitting him. I really don't remember what happened, if a teacher broke it up or what.

I don't even remember if any of us got in trouble. I do remember that I broke the first kid's nose. His dad came over to our place and wanted my dad to pay the doctor bill. It's interesting that I remember the fight but not what happened afterward. My dad was proud of me for protecting myself, but Mom wasn't so happy."

"Had you been in any fights before that?"

"No, I didn't want to fight. I would run and tell a teacher or someone. I was sort of the slow, fat kid. It was only after graduation, when I went into the army, that I lost that fat. I didn't want to fight. I guess I was afraid. I thought about running, but it was too late. That kid grabbed me. Like I said, I was slow. I got into a few fights after that a few years later, after I graduated. No one bothered me in school after that. I think they respected me because I broke his nose.

"I remember after I met Robin, my wife, we were in a bar and this guy who'd had too much tried to put the move on Robin. I hit him. The police came, and he was just sitting there, just sitting on the floor. The police already knew him and took him out. Nothing was said about me. I was just protecting Robin and myself. I had to protect us."

"You had to protect yourself?"

"I can't let anybody take advantage of me or us."

"The bullies in school and the guy in the bar were taking advantage of you. The first time we met you told me the guy feeding the machine was taking advantage of you. You have to protect yourself from anybody taking advantage of you."

Edward didn't feel great about standing up for himself, but he didn't feel bad about it either. As is typical in these therapy sessions, he was still in a trance, sitting at the edge of his chair clasping his knee as we talked, so I turned the drumming back on with the suggestion, "Go back to the bicycle rack and let the wisdom and understanding of your adult self help your younger self understand your feelings."

After a few moments of silence, Edward said, "My younger self was afraid that he wouldn't be so lucky the next time." He believed that breaking the other boy's nose was only an accident.

Edward's manner had changed a bit since the first time I had seen him. He wasn't the defensive, tough guy who first came in to see me anymore, and he was more open to revealing himself, the expected result of trance induced by the yes-set. Yet he ended treatment after completing the three sessions required by his employer. He was still blaming others for his anger. I believed that we had accomplished something, as seen in Edward's change of attitude in therapy, but knew there was more work ahead for him. So I wasn't surprised when I heard from him two years later, when he phoned for an appointment.

SAME ISSUE, DIFFERENT STORY

During the two years since I had first seen him, Edward had been fired from his job because of another altercation and had found new employment. But now his problem was that his wife, Robin, was about to leave him because of his temper. He had recently been charged with threatening someone in a road-rage incident, and this had greatly embarrassed and frightened her, as she had been in the car at the time and had experienced this before. But this time it was different because Jeff, their three-year-old grandson, had been in the car with them and had been terrified by his grandfather's explosive temper. She told Edward that he'd either have to make some changes or she'd leave him.

His wife's threatening to leave him worked to push him to face his problem. This time Edward seemed ready to own up to his behavior, yet he also felt greatly humiliated. I could understand that his wife's threat no doubt had added to his feelings of inadequacy, which in turn made him more entrenched in his belief that he was being harassed by others. Though he had made a commitment to use his willpower to hold his temper, he still experienced feelings of intense, uncontrollable rage. It's been my experience that willpower alone is not enough to change one's behavior, and Edward would eventually fail in holding his temper, probably sooner rather than later. I believe that at some level he knew that he couldn't manage his anger. At least he had the good sense to seek therapy, and that was a start.

We initially reviewed his experience of two years earlier, the first time he came to see me. We began with the relaxation exercise, and I requested again that he use it at least once a day at home. Edward again recalled the bicycle rack fight and breaking the other kid's nose, and the fight in the bar with the guy who was coming on to his wife. These stories remained quite vivid to him, so I suggested that he return to the bicycle rack and then go back even further. I had him sit as he did before, at the edge of his chair with his back straight and his left hand clasping his left knee, his right hand resting on top of his right thigh. It was apparent that he remembered the posture, the Lady of Cholula. I then turned on the recorded drumming. In this way Edward's mind remained alert in seeking answers.

After the fifteen minutes of drumming ended, Edward reported his experience. He told me he'd gone back and recalled what had happened when the two bullies confronted him at the bicycle rack, but then he went back even further:

"Hmm . . . I haven't thought of the ninth-grade lawn in years. I wonder if schools still have such lawns for one class. It's a small grass courtyard where just the ninth-graders were allowed to hang out before they graduate from middle school and go on to high school."

I repeated what Edward was saying, but put it in the present tense to deepen his trance memory. I had restarted the drumming CD. "You are on the ninth-grade lawn, a place set aside especially for you. You are there on the lawn. What are you doing? Take your time. What is happening?"

"I'm just sitting there on the wall at the edge of the lawn. One of the bullies comes toward me. He grabs my cap and runs. I get up and take a few steps after him. I feel like I'm moving in slow motion. I stop. What's the use of chasing him? I can't catch him. I don't know what to do. I'm in a panic. I feel like crying, but I know I can't." Edward stops for a moment, then adds, "I feel sick to my stomach."

After a moment, I interjected, "What's happening now?"

"He throws the cap to another kid who runs behind me. I turn around, and he throws it back to the first kid. I take a few steps in that direction, but I'm too slow, and I know I can't get it. I look around and wish a teacher would come by."

"Stay with that feeling, feel the sick feeling in your stomach. Stay with that feeling, and have your adult self go back and be with your younger self. With all the wisdom and understanding of your adult self, help your younger self understand. Take a few moments to find the best words to describe how you feel."

"Afraid, panicked. I feel like I want to cry."

"With the wisdom of your adult self, what are you afraid of?"

"Afraid I will not get my cap back."

"Afraid you will not get your cap back. Stay with that feeling. Stay with the feeling of panic. Take it deeper."

"I'm afraid that I will not get my cap back. I'm afraid I might cry. I don't know what to do. They're making a fool out of me. Everyone is laughing at me."

"Your adult self can see your younger self. What does he see?"

"He sees a fat kid just standing there. He can't do anything."

"Describe him more."

"His arms are hanging at his sides. They look long, hanging almost to his knees."

"Now take time to let your adult self be with your younger self. You know your younger self better than anyone else. Put yourself in your younger self and tell me how he feels."

"He feels like crying, but he knows he can't. If he cried everyone would really laugh at him. He feels so stupid, not being able to do anything. He looks like a fool, like a fat ape standing there with his arms hanging."

"He feels like a fool. Everyone is laughing at him. He doesn't know what to do. He feels like a fool. Stay with that feeling, feeling foolish. As an adult, you can feel that feeling of not knowing what to do. You can feel like crying for your younger self. Just feel your shoulders sagging, your arms hanging so low. Feel the humiliation of your younger self, how humiliated your adult self feels for your younger self. Now take a few breaths while experiencing that humiliation, the feeling of wanting to cry. As you come back to your adult self, wonder when you made that change in your life, the change, the decision to not let anyone make a fool out of you."

Edward had remained in trance during this entire discussion, a trance induced and maintained by the yes-set. His deliberation on how to answer my questions took him even deeper into trance.

A deeper level of fear was the fear of being the fool. The fear of being the fool was likely what eventually drove Edward to fight back. Remembering when he made the decision to fight back would clarify for him the connection with his explosive temper.

THE FEAR OF BEING MADE THE FOOL

Edward was quite good at going into a trance; in fact, simply recalling a previous trance experience would quickly take him there. During our next session, after relaxing with his hands on his center of harmony while I did the same, I suggested, "Lie down on the couch with the back of your left wrist lying on your forehead. This posture is for going into the underworld of your unconscious mind."

This is the third of the four postures I use regularly in therapy, the Jivaro Underworld posture, though I wasn't ready to give Edward this kind of information this early in our work. Instead, I lay back in my recliner, modeling the posture, as Edward lay on the couch. I started the recorded drumming and prompted, "Go back to the fight at the bicycle rack. Remember that for a moment you looked around to see if you could see a teacher and there weren't any. Let your adult self be with your younger self. Your adult self knows your younger self better than anyone else. Feel the panic in your younger self. Feel the fear of the bullies making a fool out of you. Those feelings are with you. The bully grabs you, and you fight back. After the fight you are afraid that if it happens again you might not be so lucky as to win . . . Now you are at the bar with your wife. You feel much more confident when you hit the drunk who is coming on to your wife. In between these episodes your attitude has changed. You have found the confidence to not let anyone make a fool out of you . . . Relive the experience."

After fifteen minutes of drumming, Edward sat up: "I went into the army for two years. I really changed in the army. I lost a lot of weight. I guess it happened from the first day. At that point I became a fighting man, fighting for 'truth, justice, and the American way.'" Edward sat at attention at the edge of the chair and saluted with a grin on his face.

It was apparent there were two sides to Edward: the part of him that fights back, fearing that if he doesn't he'll appear foolish, and the "fat kid" who can't fight back and who did feel foolish—his shadow self. As therapy progressed, these two parts would have to be addressed. Though Edward's fatness and fear of being foolish were likely the result of external influences—perhaps his mother encouraged him to eat too much or he felt abandoned as a child and he tried to fill that empty feeling by eating—at this point in therapy he seemed ready to take responsibility for both parts.

EXPLORING GUILT

Edward was used to blaming his anger on others. Now he realized he had to take some responsibility for it. Most important to many men is being strong and protective. Edward had seen his anger as a strength, something he used to protect himself and his family. When he lost his job he briefly felt guilty for failing his family, but then he quickly found a new and even better-paying job.

A newspaper cartoon that he showed me at the next session triggered a little guilt, yet it was not great because again Edward interpreted what he did as protecting the family. The cartoon showed the road rage of a man who was sticking his head out a car window screaming. The head was much bigger than the car, with a gaping mouth and a forked tongue sticking out. Even though the cartoon was in black and white, we both saw or described the tongue as red. Guilt over being a crazy, angry man was very short-lived. Guilt over not being a gentleman was meaningless because Edward equated being a gentleman with being weak. Guilt over scaring his wife, Robin, and especially his three-year-old grandson, Jeff, was somewhat more meaningful to him, but imagining or exploring what his rage would mean to his grandson was only speculation as far as Edward was concerned, since the boy could not express himself, and he admitted he scared Robin. Such talk in therapy was getting us nowhere. I needed to create a therapeutic experience that would allow Edward to really get in touch with his deeper feelings.

At his next session Edward said that his wife had told him that their daughter, Stacy, had dropped her son off at a babysitter's rather than bring him over to his grandparents' house after she had learned that her mother had threatened to leave Edward because of his temper. Stacy was about six months pregnant with her second child and needed Robin's help to care for little Jeff. This brought up for Stacy her childhood feelings about her father's rage. Edward had not been in touch with the fact that his anger scared his daughter, but not bringing their grandson over when she needed help made him angry. His response was, "Oh, come on now, I never hurt my daughter; she has no reason to be afraid of me!" I responded by playing for Edward a recording of the Chenille Sisters' "I Lie in the Dark":

> I lie in the dark and I hear them shout
> I don't understand what they're fighting about
> If I cover my ears I won't hear what they say
> If I close my eyes it will all go away . . .
> It makes me afraid when he gets so mad
> and sometimes I wish that he wasn't my dad . . .
> So why do they yell, don't they know how I cry
> It makes me feel like there's nothing inside . . .
> Forever and ever they battle and bleed
> Night after night it's forever the same[1]

Music connects with the right brain. People stay with songs like a story, maybe even more so. This song struck a chord in Edward. Upon returning home after this session, he told Robin about the song. Robin then told him how their daughter would cry in fear at night when Edward would lose his temper. She and Stacy had always been afraid to tell him because doing so would probably set him off on yet another tirade. Edward felt his anger rising, but he controlled himself, instead saying, "I've never hurt either one of you." But Robin interjected, "I know you haven't hurt us physically, but I sure thought at times you were close to it." At this, Edward broke down in front of Robin. He finally felt guilty—a guilt that caused him to take responsibility for his anger.

At the next session I offered that usually beneath anger there are other feelings; in his case, guilt. "Guilt, such as the guilt of causing Stacy to fear you, can cause a person to react in one of two ways: to explode in anger or to cry. Which is more effective? Even though men are not supposed to cry, crying brings you closer to others, while anger pushes them away. Feeling bad about scaring Robin and Stacy is healthy. Anger makes any situation much worse. Crying is healing, though. You learned to be angry. Let's begin to unlearn it."

It was time to go deeper into Edward's unconscious mind so he could understand the source of his anger and his feelings of guilt. Feeling taken advantage of was an evident source, but there was something deeper. I instructed him, "When the drumming starts, lie down on the couch and rest the back of your left hand on your forehead. But first I want you to stand tall with your hands resting on your center of harmony to relax and clear your mind of extraneous thoughts. Feel the healing and cleansing with each breath." Nothing else was said, and I did not use the recorded drumming while he stood in the Bear Spirit posture since he was quite accomplished in going into a trance. After about five minutes I started the drumming and joined him, lying down in the prescribed position. I offered the suggestion to "take your anger further back in time." After fifteen minutes, I asked Edward to report his experience.

"I used to get so angry with my mother," he said. "I'm not sure why. She was always nice. Everyone loved her. When she would get on my case about something, she wasn't mean, but she would infuriate me."

"What would she say? What do you hear?"

"'I asked you this morning to mow the grass. After all I do for you, can't you help around here a little?'"

"After all I do for you."

"Yeah, 'after all I do for you.'"

"Those are infuriating words. You didn't ask to be born."

"Yeah, that's what I would say sometimes."

"Has Stacy ever heard you use those words, 'after all I have done for you'? Have you ever put that guilt trip on her or Robin?"

"No, I don't think so. I hate those words. I thought they were unfair."

"Well, good. Those guilt-tripping words *are* infuriating, but there are other things you do say. When you tell them, 'You know I would never hurt you,' you are telling them they should not be afraid of you, that they are wrong in being afraid of you, suggesting that they should feel guilty about their fear of you. I wonder how they feel about your telling them that. "

"Robin gets irritated."

"She hears you as not understanding her feelings."

Edward now understood the anger triggered in him by the guilt trip his mother had put on him, but he still thought that it was unfair that Robin and Stacy were afraid of him.

Over the next couple of sessions, Edward became more and more aware of Robin and Stacy's fear, of how his wife would placate him, trying to keep the peace, and when she failed, she would yell at him to calm down. Stacy would just get quiet, look scared, and hold her three-year-old tightly between her knees with her arms wrapped around him and his head resting on her pregnant belly. Edward realized that the boy would never come to him spontaneously, and if he tried to get him to come to him the boy would run to his mommy. Running to Stacy had become the child's habit around Edward, who told me these things with tears in his eyes.

Edward missed the next couple of sessions because Stacy was almost due. Lilly, the new baby, was about a week old when Edward finally came in. He had seen her once in the hospital, but his daughter had not yet taken the baby by their house, as Robin was apprehensive about having Edward around the newborn. For this reason, Robin had gone once, by herself, to visit Stacy and the new grandchild. This made for a new urgency in therapy, as Edward knew he needed to learn how to cultivate their trust if he wanted to spend time with his new granddaughter.

THE CHIHUAHUA

Edward was still not completely in touch with the effects his anger had on others. He complained about Robin's protectiveness around their daughter and grandchildren, especially Jeff.

"When she tells me that Stacy grabs Jeff to comfort him around me, she doesn't understand that her grabbing him only makes the boy's fear worse. It tells him he should be afraid." Though I admitted that there was perhaps some truth to what Edward was saying, trying to convince his daughter that she was wrong to do what she did with her son just wouldn't work. What would work better would be for Edward to show them that he understood their feelings.

"All your barking is getting you nowhere," I flat out told him. "I think it's a good time for you to find the right spirit guide to help you understand Robin and Stacy's feelings. These guides are those you find in the images and characters you experience in your imagination, dreams, and trance experiences." I suggested using the Lady of Cholula posture. We started, as usual, in the Bear Spirit to relax and for ego strengthing. After a few minutes I started the recorded drumming, and we both sat down at the edge of our chairs. After about five minutes, Edward interrupted the drumming. He was quick to catch on to the image I had suggested earlier when I referred to his barking:

"The first thing I saw was a barking dog, a little dog like a Chihuahua, barking and snarling. I knew it wasn't going to hurt me. When I stepped toward the dog, it quickly backed away. But when I turned and walked away from it, it came after me. It would nip at my heels and wouldn't leave me alone, but still, I knew it wouldn't hurt me. I was walking with Robin, and when it snarled, she jumped behind me, and the dog jumped at her. I thought she was being silly, but I also knew I had to protect her, so I kicked the dog and it went away yelping."

"So the yapping Chihuahua is your spirit guide. What is it showing you? You know you need not be afraid of him, yet Robin was afraid of him and sought your protection. You protected her, just as Stacy protects Jeff."

"But it's ridiculous to be afraid of such a small dog."

"Why do small dogs generally make so much noise?"

"I think they know they're vulnerable, but their barking makes them feel big."

"The little dog wants you to be intimidated by him, and sometimes it works. At least his bark intimidates Robin, and maybe Jeff would be intimidated by him too, as small as he is."

The drumming recording was still playing, and Edward remained in the posture, sitting tall at the edge of his chair. I suggested, "Let's take this further. Become the Chihuahua." When in a trance, changing the direction of the experience can be guided verbally without changing the posture. "Robin is intimidated by you. What happens?"

"I'm so small, she shouldn't be intimidated."

"But you're barking to intimidate her. You want her to be intimidated. That's why you're barking."

"Oh . . . " Edward was beginning to catch on.

"You want her to think your bite would hurt."

The session ended, leaving Edward with much to think about.

When Edward arrived for his next session, I had an idea. I suggested that we use another posture that I had not used previously in his therapy, the Olmec Prince, a metamorphosis posture, so that Edward could gain the knowledge that would come from becoming his spirit guide, the Chihuahua. I had Edward sit cross-legged on the floor and reach out to place the knuckles of his hands on the floor before him. Usually a person in this posture experiences his arms as forelegs, and Edward was no different.

After the initial ritual of standing with our hands on our center of harmony to relax and quiet his mind, I turned on the drumming. He then sat on the floor and placed the knuckles of his fists on the floor in front of him just as I was doing. Edward soon interrupted the drumming.

"I wasn't small, I was fat, but I still felt small compared to the bullies. To them, my bark meant nothing, but my bite did. I broke one kid's nose. Then I didn't feel so small. I wouldn't bite Robin, and I feel small with her. I feel strong when I bark at her because I know she feels intimidated." It was obvious that he had been doing a lot of thinking during the week prior to this session, but the ecstatic trance posture helped him clarify his thoughts at a deeper level.

"Is there an alternative?" I asked. With this insight, the following week we used the final posture of the five I use in therapy, the Feathered Serpent, to bring about the death of his barking self. I demonstrated the stance of the posture: "Stand tall with the backs of your hands resting on your hips, with your elbows extending outward, away from your body." He followed along, and I asked him what he thought the posture expressed. At first he mentioned being angry and defiant. I asked him if he had seen it before, and he described his mother standing this way when she scolded him. I said that "angry" and "defiant" might be too strong a way to describe the intent of this posture, but *determination* might be a better word—that your mother was determined to get you to do something. He thought maybe, but it still felt like scolding to him. I then suggested, "But it is you, not your mother, who is standing that way now. What do *you* feel?" Edward agreed that he did not feel like he was scolding anyone, but that he was feeling determined.

With this introduction to the new posture, we both started out in the Bear Spirit for a few minutes to relax and quiet our minds. Then, as the drumming started, we both stood in the Feathered Serpent posture. I added the suggestion that he imagine he was sitting on the floor as he did the previous week, but with the barking Chihuahua facing him. After the fifteen minutes of drumming ended, I asked him what he had experienced in trance.

"The dog barked and yipped for a while, but eventually it quieted down and actually came over and laid its head in my lap."

"What do you think happened? Why?"

"I guess I wasn't intimidating to him."

"Yes. You were more his size by sitting on the floor, and your fists on the floor in front of you were more like front legs and not fisted hands. He could relate to you as a four-legged, but most important was your relaxed breathing, something that animals very quickly pick up on. The way you were sitting and your breathing was telling him that you understood how a big human like you can be intimidating to a small dog. You showed him that you understood and that he could trust you."

His Chihuahua spirit guide had taught him an important lesson, the lesson that relaxed breathing communicates trust and is not intimidating, a lesson that he began incorporating within himself with the use of the Feathered Serpent posture for death and rebirth.

INCORPORATING BIOFEEDBACK

Edward came to the next session expressing disappointment. Stacy had visited her parents and had brought Jeff and the new baby. "I did my best to stay calm," he said. "I don't think I raised my voice once, but I could still see that Jeff was scared of me. I put my arms out to him, and he ran to his mother. She put her arms out to grab him without even looking at me. It made me mad that Stacy didn't tell Jeff to go to me, but I don't think I showed it." Edward's sensitivity to their being afraid of him was a good sign, though, a minor breakthrough, as he was finally sensing the effects his temper had on others.

Edward had learned how to cultivate internal calmness to a degree, but it could still be deeper. Sometimes I use biofeedback in therapy, and I had an idea in mind for Edward. Though he would probably not have the opportunity to hold his new granddaughter for a while, preparing him for holding her would open the door to new possibilities in therapy. It seemed like a good time to use biofeedback. I had him stand with his hands on his center of harmony, and I turned on the drumming at a soft volume. I attached the two terminals of the galvanic skin response (GSR) modality to Edward's fingers. GSR measures electrical conductivity between two fingers and is very sensitive to changes in skin moisture due to changes in body tension or anxiety. It is often used to teach a person deep relaxation. Having him stand in the Bear Spirit posture brought him more quickly to a state of deep relaxation as now noted in the drop in pitch of the biofeedback tone. In this case, I wanted him to see the difference between his loving and patient self versus his angry, tense self.

"Imagine yourself holding Lilly, holding her gently in your arms. She is sleeping quietly. Rock her gently. Feel her warmth. Feel her soft breathing and soft skin. You are sitting back, feeling good. As you relax deeper and deeper, holding Lilly in your arms, listen to the tone of the biofeedback going lower and lower. As you relax deeper and deeper, the tone becomes lower and lower. See how deeply you can relax by bringing the tone as low as you can make it."

The pitch of the tone steadily dropped as Edward concentrated on the image. When the tone began to level out, I changed the suggestion: "Now, Lilly begins to wake up. She starts to whimper. She is squirming and begins to cry louder." Immediately, Edward's tension increased, and the pitch of the tone shot up.

"Now, stay relaxed. Focus on relaxing your arms as much as possible. Focus on breathing slowly and evenly. As you relax deeper and deeper, look at Lilly and ask her silently, *What are you trying to say? What are you trying to tell me?* Think about the different possibilities— a wet diaper, hungry, scared, uncomfortable because of just waking up. Realize how when you first wake up you may feel different feelings of discomfort, especially if you are in a strange place and experiencing different smells. Realize how people smell different, and you are a different smell to Lilly. There are many possible reasons Lilly is crying. Look at her with a real sense of patience, asking these questions and thinking of the many possible answers. As you watch her in this way, notice how her crying drops back to being just a whimper. Notice how your patience and confidence in holding her feels reassuring to her so that she does not have to cry." Again the biofeedback tone had been dropping as Edward deepened his relaxation.

After a minute or two, again I changed the suggestion: "Now, change your thinking to, *Oh no, Lilly is crying, what am I going to do? I hate it when babies cry! Why do they always have to cry?* Notice how quickly the tone again begins to go up. Notice how quickly just changing the way you think makes the tone go up or down, how quickly the tension in your body changes. Babies are very sensitive to such tension. When they feel tension, they feel insecure, scared, and will cry. When you stay relaxed and show Lilly a sense of relaxed confidence, she will not cry loudly but cry quietly, only to communicate to you that she is uncomfortable in some way."

When the biofeedback session ended, I reminded Edward, "Though Stacy and Robin may not be ready for you to hold Lilly, keep this in mind when you do have a chance to hold her. Think about your body tension, your patience and relaxation, and notice how Lilly responds to you. From my experience, noticing these feelings within you can work almost magically, and when others are unable to quiet a baby, you will find that you can do it easily. It just takes some practice and definitely an awareness of your own feelings."

At the next session Edward started out by telling me that he once again tried putting his arms out to invite Jeff to come to him, and again Jeff ran away from him and to his mother. He did say that he felt a greater sense of calmness as he put his arms out to his grandson, though. While telling his story I could see that he was having a hard time catching his breath. He was on the verge of crying. Crying is something that men generally can't accept because they are conditioned to believe it's a sign of weakness. I had already explained to Edward that crying is not weak, but strong, and much more effective than anger. "Crying makes you feel much more like partners, not enemies."

"I think I cried once before, when Robin miscarried before Stacy was born. I remember Robin holding me and how good it felt. Robin was crying too. We felt more like partners back then."

"You don't feel like either Robin or Stacy is encouraging Jeff to come to you. They are not being your partners in this. That hurts. Wouldn't it feel good if they tried to teach Jeff that he could trust you? But they don't trust like the Chihuahua trusts you."

I thought that Edward could once again benefit from using the Feathered Serpent death-rebirth posture to incorporate within his unconscious mind what he had learned from the Chihuahua, as well as the feeling of trust he had learned as a result of the biofeedback session. After a few minutes of standing in the Bear Spirit, I turned on the drumming recording, and we both stood up with the backs of our hands on our hips.

At the end of the drumming, Edward related his experience:

"I quickly felt very relaxed and quiet inside. I was in the living room sitting with Robin, Stacy, and Lilly. Jeff was running around. Jeff ran by me and brushed against my knee or backed up against my knee, but I was sitting back relaxed and did nothing, and Jeff looked up at me and just ran on as he had been doing. He seemed relaxed running into me and didn't seem frightened of me."

"Great. You didn't do anything. You didn't put your arms out. Putting your arms out has become a trigger for his fear."

The following week, Edward said that he and Robin had visited Stacy and her family. Everyone sat together for a few minutes except for Chuck, Stacy's husband, who paced around. He then took Jeff, announced that they were going to Home Depot to get something he needed for the deck he was building and then left. The conversation went dead, and Stacy could see how Robin was hurt that Jeff was not staying for their visit. Edward got up and said that he was walking home. Robin started getting up too, but Stacy put her hand on her mom's arm, saying, "Let him go; it'll do him good." The walk to their house was about two miles, and Robin got home soon after Edward. When she walked in, Edward expressed anger, but it was within reason and directed at Chuck. Edward could see that Robin was hurt too by Chuck taking Jeff and leaving during the visit. She seemed to realize that Edward was trying. Edward felt supported by Robin's understanding, which helped him stay calm.

LEARNING ABOUT THE POSTURES

Upon hearing this I thought it was important to reinforce the experience of the previous week, both by using the posture again and by beginning to explain the deeper meaning of the postures. I began, "Let's try again what we did last week with the posture we used then. "When I first began using the postures for this kind of work, each posture was given a name. The one we used last week is called the Feathered Serpent. Where it comes from is, I think, very interesting." I then told Edward about Felicitas Goodman, ecstatic trance, and her discovery that different body postures had specific effects on the trance experience. I told him about the origins of the Feathered Serpent, as well as the other postures we had used—the Bear Spirit, the Lady of Cholula, and the Jivaro. Edward was listening with interest.

"The Feathered Serpent is for producing a death-rebirth experience—the death of some part of you that is not working for you and the birth of a healthier part of you. The birth of the innocent, healthier part of you is sometimes referred to as *soul retrieval,* which refers to retrieving an innocent part of yourself that was lost a long time ago. So let's use the Feathered Serpent posture again. Take with you your experiences with the Chihuahua and Jeff bumping into your knee. First stand in the Bear Spirit posture for a few minutes to relax and quiet your mind." Then, as I started drumming, we both stood in the Feathered Serpent posture.

After the fifteen minutes the drumming ended, and Edward related the following trance experience of recalling an actual experience of his past.

"Robin and I were in a restaurant. Sitting across from us was a family, a boy about Jeff's age sitting between his grandfather and mother, and across the table was the grandmother. I saw the grandfather helping the boy cut his meat. As I watched, the boy looked up and saw me watching him. I quickly ducked down behind my menu. When I looked up again he again noticed me, and I again ducked. The third time the boy smiled, and I had to smile back. I wish Jeff wasn't afraid of me like that."

I laughed. "Young children love that game of peekaboo. When you play hard to get, they are quickly hooked. That's a game you can play with Jeff. Look at Jeff, watch him, and as soon as he sees you looking at him, turn your head away quickly. It may not take long for Jeff to catch on, and it would be hard for him not to be enticed by this game. Don't try to get him to come to you, and don't go to him, but play hard-to-get this way. Depending on how afraid he is of you, it may take some patience on your part to get him to play along, but I expect that it won't take that long. Stacy doesn't need to know what you're doing—it'll be between you and Jeff."

Edward liked this suggestion and was ready to try again. With my support he was having some success with exercising patience. His daughter didn't seem to be aware of how hard Edward was trying, but Robin was catching on. For years Stacy had been collecting fears and resentments toward her father. Chuck was an even bigger problem. Wanting to protect Stacy and Jeff, one evening he told Stacy that she was not to visit her mother when her father was at home. What Chuck said got back to Edward through Robin, and he once again lost his temper. Robin probably should not have told Edward this, but because she knew he was trying to change, she hoped she could tell him and that he could deal with it. In any case, he lost a lot of ground with Robin. His rage, a disruptive cry for help, set him back.

When Edward told me this story, I offered, "Wow, just at the time you were trying to change and be more gentle, everything goes wrong. No one seems to have noticed how hard you are trying . . . Actually, your wife knows, and I expect that your daughter would know eventually and probably her husband, too. Maybe they're just impatient, or maybe they don't believe you can do it. Maybe they think it should be easy for you to change."

STALKING

Though Edward had been showing considerable patience, I knew it wouldn't hurt and would only benefit him to find a deeper level of strength, to find another spirit guide that could show him the strength of what I call *stalking,* using a sense of quiet, attentive focus on what needs to be done in a situation. The sequence of three postures for soul retrieval—of divining an answer, of going into the underworld to give it a chance to develop, and then a death-rebirth posture to integrate it—could lead Edward to a new level of strength that comes from focusing on other people rather than self-centeredly giving all one's attention to one's own pain.

I suggested that he start out by standing in the Bear Spirit posture to find calmness within and to quiet his mind. Then I suggested that he sit at the edge of his chair in the Lady of Cholula posture, to find a spirit guide that could teach him the strength of stalking. After the drumming ended, Edward related his experience:

"A few weeks ago I saw a brief YouTube video of a mongoose and a cobra. The mongoose was standing out of reach of the cobra, but every so often it would lunge at the cobra, then jump away, sometimes wandering off for a break in the confrontation. After a while, the mongoose got ahold of the cobra just behind its head. It carefully stalked the cobra until it got it. I could feel the mongoose flowing quietly with the swaying of the cobra waiting for an opening to lunge."

"Take with you that feeling of waiting quietly for the right time," I said. "It's all about timing."

At our next session I had a story to tell Edward:

"So far in these sessions we have used several different postures for going into trance while listening to the beating of a drum. Ecstatic trance very often leads you to find what we would call a spirit guide who has something to teach you. In your first experience your guides were the two bullies, and in a later session the guide was your mother, from whom you learned about guilt trips. Another guide was the Chihuahua, and then the mongoose and cobra. You have learned a lot from these guides.

"You've probably noticed the four leather shields I have hanging here. They are some of my personal spirit guides. I have an adopted daughter who is part Native American. She is now in her forties, but when she was young I used to enjoy reading her Native American stories, and as I read them I learned a lot about myself. One of my favorites is *Seven Arrows,* by Hyemeyohsts Storm, a Cheyenne. It taught me a lot. In our white-man culture we often say, 'You can't teach an old dog new tricks.' I then learned that wasn't true. We *are* here to learn new tricks, and we learn them throughout our entire lives. One thing I learned from Storm was about the Medicine Wheel, and that each direction of the wheel has something to say to us. East is represented by the birds; South by the smaller animals; West by the carnivorous animals, the dogs, cats, and bears; and North by the animals with antlers. According to Storm, when we are born our parents go on a vision quest to find us a name. The name is of an animal who tells us from which direction we were born.

"What I found beautiful in this story is that we are to search throughout our lives in each direction to eventually find our four names. In other words, the Native American idea is that we spend our lives searching, learning, and growing. I have found my four medicine shields, and I am still learning. When I use ecstatic trance for myself, I start the ritual by calling the spirits of each direction.

"When you think about your spirit guides, yours represent two of the directions. The Chihuahua is of the West, and the mongoose is of the South. As we continue using ecstatic trance in therapy, I would like to start the ritual by calling on the spirits of the six directions."

Edward seemed amenable to the idea and even excited by it, so I began by calling the spirits of the six directions: "Spirits of the East, of spring and the sunrise, of the beginning of life, we honor you; bring us your wisdom." I took a pinch of cornmeal in my fingers and offered it in that direction. I continued, offering a pinch of cornmeal to each direction: "Spirits of the South, of the middle of day, of warmth and growth, we honor you; join us and bring us your wisdom . . . Spirits of the West, of autumn and the sunset, of the harvest and our productive years of life, we honor you; join us and bring us your wisdom . . . Spirits of the North, of nighttime and of Winter, spirits of our elder years, of hibernation, sleep, and death in preparation for a new birth at spring, we honor you; join us and bring us your wisdom . . . Spirits of the universe who placed Earth in a distance from the Sun that sustains life, that brings us night and day and the seasons of the year, that brings us the tides of the oceans, we honor you. Join us and bring us your wisdom . . . Spirits of our great Mother Earth who sustains us, who breathes such that we have oxygen to breathe and who provides us with necessary warmth, fire from burning wood, wool clothing from sheep, and warmth from the Sun, we honor you. Bring us your wisdom and join us."

With this calling of the spirits, and after a few minutes of standing in the Bear Spirit posture to bring strength and to quiet our minds, I indicated that we should sit on the floor with legs crossed and knuckles on the floor in front of us in the Olmec Prince posture, so that Edward could experience the stalking strength of the mongoose. I then began drumming.

After fifteen minutes, the drumming ended, and Edward related his experience:

"I was crouched not far from the cobra. I could feel my legs trembling, and I was ready to spring. All of my attention was on the cobra. In looking back now, there was nothing else. All my attention was in that one direction, like when I'm driving over the mountain at night, watching for the gleaming eyes of deer. I've hit a couple of deer at night so I'm very wary. My eyes are constantly scanning back and forth, watching both sides of the road. I can feel that energy of being so focused on the cobra, ready to jump back in any direction, at any moment, and ready to spring at the cobra's neck."

I suggested, "The energy of stalking, of being prepared for anything, is very powerful, more powerful than anger. Anger is a loss of control, a loss of being aware and prepared. In anger your energy flies off in all directions, though you still may not be aware of anything else around you."

The next session seemed to be the right time to incorporate this stalking energy Edward had connected with, so I suggested using the Feathered Serpent posture. While in trance Edward took the experience back to the mongoose and cobra confrontation, but this time he focused on the swaying energy of the cobra. After the drumming ended he related his experience:

"I first found myself watching and swaying to the rhythm of the cobra, the cobra's energy of stalking, slower than the drum, then the rhythm of Jeff running through the living room into the dining room, in a circle, into the kitchen and back out into the living room. Though he can be hyperactive and running around does not feel very rhythmic, his brief reappearance into and through the living room felt rhythmic. I would look up and follow him through the living room with my eyes. I think he felt me watching him, and it became a game with him. We were both smiling as he would run through the living room and frowning as he ran out."

I mentioned that the snake for some tribes is a spirit of the Earth.

It was clear that Edward was starting to look at the world differently. Whereas at the beginning of therapy he was very self-absorbed, caught up in his own feelings of others taking advantage of him, now he was thinking beyond himself, of how others feel—Robin and Stacy's fear of his anger, little Jeff's fear and habit of running to his mother, Chuck's need to protect his wife, and even Lilly's tension and relaxation in the arms of someone else. Whereas previously he was trying to control others in a very self-centered way, through rage, now he was learning that others have feelings too, and they may be different from his own. And he was finding that their feelings are valid. Though he still had much to learn, especially how to relinquish control, with his recent changes he was now capable of opening himself up to his spirit guides.

INVITING OTHERS INTO THE PROCESS

The following week Edward reported that he did have a chance to play the hard-to-get game with Jeff, and this time the boy responded well. We repeated our ecstatic trance sequence, but this time we used the Feathered Serpent death-rebirth posture, and Edward related his experience: "We were all sitting in the living room, Robin, Stacy, and Jeff, and I was in my recliner feeling relaxed and warm, just sitting there feeling very comfortable watching Jeff and occasionally looking away when he would look up. The relaxed warmth made me feel like I was at home, in a safe place, like I belonged there." Edward now felt like he was part of his family. The changes Edward needed to make were happening, even though Robin, Stacy, and Chuck seemed to be unaware of it.

Edward reported the following week that Stacy and Jeff had come for a visit, and during the visit he played peekaboo with Jeff. Just then it felt like the right time for him to put his arms out toward Jeff. Jeff stopped and looked startled, looked around, and again ran to his mother. Stacy jumped up and shouted at her father, "Don't ever do that again!" and stormed out of the house. Robin looked at Edward with tears in her eyes and shook her head with a sigh. She could feel Edward's frustration. She understood both Edward and her daughter, and she didn't know what to do. At least this time Edward felt Robin's emotional support. He was more scared than angry, scared and hurt for both himself and for Robin, and Stacy's anger scared him too. Rather than feeling angry in response, he felt an inner quietness. He was numb, beyond anger. This inner quietness was focused on the thought *What should I do?* I could feel his strength growing within him and suggested, "Your growing frustration feels like a focused strength, like a cat stalking its prey in silence."

We talked a bit about what Edward might do. He realized that he couldn't get the boy to come to him, so he was open to considering new possibilities. I asked him, "Would your wife, would your daughter come in for a session? I could explain to them that changing a strongly engrained habit takes time and emotional support." I thought that Edward was well enough along his path of change that he was ready to include others in the family in therapy.

Edward doubted that his daughter would come, but he saw the wisdom in trying to get his wife to come. I explained, "From my past experience in similar situations, your wife might possibly go on and on, telling me everything bad about you, and the session would require tremendous patience on your part, but if you are able to remain patient and let me listen to her, your patience could impress her. If you begin to say something I might just put my hand up to stop you. Be ready for that. If it should go that way, I'd like to hear her out first."

Robin did come in for the next session, and in fact for the next two sessions. Stacy's work schedule would not permit her coming. In the first session, as expected, Robin expressed great frustration and resentment.

"Edward is such a hothead and doesn't get along with anybody," she said. "He hasn't physically abused me or Stacy, but we still have been abused by him." She went on, taking up the whole hour with her complaints. I attempted to cut her off a couple of times, but she pushed right on through. I ended the session with the proposition that in the next session I would do more of the talking, adding, "Let's consider what we can do to help Edward change. You know he does want to change."

Robin snapped back, "What do you mean he wants to change? He just wants us to think that."

I put my hand up and stood up to end the session, "Let's consider that at the next session." I could see Edward squirming in his seat, but he did a pretty good job of staying quiet and just listening. As they left I had a moment alone with Edward while Robin went into the restroom. I said to him, "You did a good job. That took a lot of strength to listen to what Robin had to say."

At the next session I began with, "Let me tell you a story. This one guy, in a situation not a whole lot different from Edward's, wanted to change. He was determined to stay calm and collected. But each time a situation would come up he would think, *No one trusts me,* or *No one believes me,* or *They are making a fool out of me.* At work he would try to point out how the job could be done more efficiently and better, but no one took him seriously; no one would listen. At home the situation was about the same. So in these situations he tried his best to stay calm, but his thinking was still *No one trusts me,* or *She's making a fool out of me.* His frustration would build and build. And guess what would happen? He would explode. Using willpower is not enough to make a change. A person has to change the way he thinks, he has to change his assumptions about the world, and this takes time, understanding, and support. I wanted you to come in so that you might learn how you can help Edward change. I do believe that he wants to change, and he is struggling to do so. It's easy for you to see or feel the tension and frustration in him even when he is quiet and trying his best to stay calm." I knew that Edward was much further ahead in changing than that. "He puts his arms out for Jeff to come to him, and you can feel the frustration building when Jeff runs to his mother. Even though Edward may say nothing, he will start to make progress only when he is able to remain calm. Jeff, like all children, is especially in tune with feelings, and he feels his grandfather's frustration even when Edward tries not to show it." It was apparent to both me and Edward that he was learning to stay calm, and that Jeff was beginning to pick up on that. In this last incident, he did not run to his mother, but walked slowly to her, not knowing what to think about his grandfather's outstretched arms.

This story was as much told for Edward's benefit as it was for Robin's. I was glad that they could hear it together. Edward went home with new resolve. He arrived at our next session grinning.

"I tried playing the hard-to-get game with Jeff again. I was sitting looking at Jeff over the top of my newspaper. He was clinging to his mom, but I had him hooked. At first he didn't smile, so I started smiling. Jeff gave me a little half-smile at first. Clinging to his mom seemed to make Jeff more reserved. Then I really frowned at him and then laughed. It didn't take long for Jeff to start laughing. Stacy was funny. She didn't know what was going on at first, but then she had a big smile on her face when she figured it out."

"I think you are getting somewhere," I told him. "Keep it up, but don't go to Jeff; let Jeff decide when he wants to come to you. Don't push it or try too hard."

"Stacy mentioned afterward to Robin that Jeff is starting to like me," he said.

"I'm guessing that Stacy and Robin have talked."

It was soon after that session that Stacy left her baby with Robin, and while Robin was babysitting she suggested that Edward hold her. "Lilly was quiet and seemed very comfortable being in my arms," Edward reported, "but I don't think that Robin saw that what I was doing was magical."

"You have plenty of time, the rest of your life, to practice and demonstrate that magic. Maybe one of those times Robin will hand you Lilly when she is fussy. That will provide you with another level of practice. With your commitment to learning this magic, it will happen."

CONFRONTING THE CONTROL FREAK

There was another element that cropped up in one of Edward's sessions that had to be faced. Sometime after Robin came to therapy with him, Edward mentioned that when he was young he went to a therapy session with his mother, who was bulimic. "I don't remember much except sometimes hearing Mom throwing up in the bathroom and Dad yelling at her, 'Don't do that; you don't have to throw up.' When I was in junior high school she was seeing a therapist for it. I remember she asked me to come to one therapy session when everyone was there, Dad and my grandparents."

"Wow, that was a long time ago. Family therapy was not greatly in vogue then."

"All I can remember is Mom yelling at Gramp, 'You always tried to control me; you never let me be me.' I can still hear those words. I guess they sort of scared me. I can't remember Mom ever being angry."

"What do you remember about Gramp?"

"I don't actually remember running away from Gramp, but I remember being scared of him. He never smiled and always seemed grumpy."

I responded with the words of his mother: "You always try to control me; you never let me be me." Those words registered with Edward.

"Yeah, Mom often complained that he was a control freak."

I added, "And as we know, controlling doesn't work, it only creates a challenge to find ways to get away with what you want to do. Did your dad stop your mom from throwing up?"

"Yeah, I mean no. When Dad told Mom not to throw up, she still did but just tried to be sneaky about it. She would binge and throw up before Dad got home, and then eat very little during dinner. I know that because I was already home from school. I don't think she thought I knew what was going on."

Therapy was beginning to delve into a new issue, that of control, or specifically, of being a control freak.

This matter of control came up at Edward's next session.

"Robin used a hammer from my shop, and I have a thing about my tools. I want to be able to find them when I need them. I found the hammer on the porch on my way out to the shop and said to Robin, 'Couldn't you put it away?' She said that she would the next time she went out by the shop and added, 'Sheeesh, what a control freak!' People hate control freaks. I guess I'm one."

"Let's again use ecstatic trance, sitting at the edge of your chair in the Lady of Cholula posture, with the question, 'What can I do differently if I find the hammer on the porch?' But first we'll call the spirits of each direction, then stand in the Bear Spirit to quiet your mind." After this part of the induction ritual I picked up my drum and started drumming as Edward sat down with a smile as he got into the posture. I added, "Maybe you will find a new spirit guide."

At the end of fifteen minutes, Edward gave this account:

"Katy, our little terrier, is well trained. The first thing I do in the morning is put out a dish of food for her. After she eats, I open the door, and she goes outside for a few minutes. She is very pregnant. The other morning I opened the door for her to go out before I fed her. She looked very confused and whined at the door. I put out the food, and when I let her back in she went to her food, and then pooped in front of her food dish. I quickly put her back outside and cleaned up the mess. After a while I let her back in, but she has made a mess in the house a couple of times ever since."

"What do you make of it?"

"She's out of control."

"Yeah, her routine was broken, and her pregnancy makes it a little more difficult. She is out of control. Finding the hammer on the porch broke your routine, and you pooped on Robin with your complaint."

Edward snorted in a quiet laugh. "But I didn't mean to change Katy's routine. I just wasn't thinking. Some mornings are that way."

"Things mess up routines. Wouldn't it be nice in those cases if shit didn't happen?"

Edward got the point, and Katy became another one of his spirit guides. We had discovered that another dimension to his anger was his need to control.

He reported at his next session that "this time when Stacy and Jeff were over, Jeff was playing on the floor with one of his trucks. I walked by and ruffled his hair. He jumped up crying and ran to his mom. I looked at her in shock, and she said to Jeff, 'Gramp was showing you that he loves you.'"

"That was a nice thing for Stacy to say, a big improvement."

"Jeff just looked at me with big eyes. I thought about how afraid I was of my grandfather. I don't want Jeff to feel that way about me."

"Give him some time. Probably your grandfather just tried too hard, tried to control you to get you to love him."

COMBATTING ROAD RAGE

Edward was making improvements, but there were still those times that he tried to control or would feel very frustrated when things didn't go his way, especially when driving. His tension and tendency to rage behind the wheel frightened Robin. He told her that his anger was with the other drivers and not with her, but that didn't seem to matter to her. She complained loudly when she came with him to therapy.

"He's doing so well with Jeff, but there's still so much anger in him. It comes out when he's driving. I can't stand driving with him. Someone always seems to cut too close in front of him or passes him going too fast, and he lets the world know. He doesn't think of the times when he cuts in front or speeds past someone else. He does the same thing. He does those things when he's mad with the other driver. It's not safe."

"But I'm just letting off steam!"

"You're being a control freak." There were those words again.

Edward's mouth fell open, but he couldn't say anything. I just grinned at him. I knew he got the message. Jeff's change in attitude toward him was very rewarding for Edward, but changing the road-rage habit was much more difficult because he had no control over other drivers.

"When was the last time you were driving faster than you probably should be, cutting in front of other cars?" I asked him.

"I was in a hurry. I was late for something; I forget what."

"You were late, not just driving that way because of some sort of reckless urge. You weren't being reckless for the thrill of it. There are many different kinds of drivers. Some may be driving fast just because they're running late. Let's go back to Katy," I suggested. "Let's use the Jivaro posture." Robin had been coming to enough sessions and had been experiencing our routine and the effects of trance for us to proceed this way even while she was in attendance. Also Edward had told her about the postures and a number of his experiences. After calling the spirits and quieting his mind with the Bear Spirit posture, he lay back on the couch with his wrist resting on his forehead as I began drumming.

Afterward, Edward told me, "After the last session with Katy, now when I get up in the morning I spend a few minutes petting her before I put her food out. I made up to her, and everything has been fine ever since."

"You took a few minutes to show her you understood her confusion or frustration, and that solved the problem—just like you can understand the other driver who might be running late and in a hurry, or even the thrill seeker, as dangerous as that is. Having empathy for and understanding others bring people together rather than causing more conflict and even wars."

SYNCHRONICITY

With each passing week Edward's games with his grandson brought Jeff closer and closer to his grandfather. Then a week came when Edward reported that Robin had commented that Jeff now was more likely to run to Edward than to her when he wanted something. When the extended family was together, Edward's focus was on Jeff, and a real bond was developing between the two of them. Edward had found a rewarding niche and was feeling appreciated by Robin, Stacy, and now even Chuck. When his daughter and her family came over, Edward spent time with Jeff, giving the others time to do things together and enjoy Stacy's new baby. Stacy had been a little concerned because of all the attention given to the baby had taken attention away from Jeff, but now Edward's focus on little Jeff solved the problem.

Yet the day came when everything came crashing down. Stacy and the kids had come over for a visit. Edward was playing happily on the floor with Jeff, who was climbing on his back, while the others were in the kitchen around the table talking. Jeff was laughing and having a great time until he slipped off his grandfather's back, sliding head first off his shoulder. With a thump his face hit the floor, and his head came up with blood dripping from his nose. He let out a scream, and Stacy came running. She grabbed Jeff, and as she ran back into the kitchen to get a wet towel she shouted back, "Dad, you need to be more careful." There was nothing Edward could say. He was devastated, and no one paid attention to his excuses or apologies. His newfound confidence was dealt a blow.

However, sometimes, as with Edward in this situation, the right thing happens at the right time in order for a lesson to be learned, for innocence to die, the death of the good feelings and trust that had recently come to be expected. This was an example of synchronicity, a concept first explained by Carl Jung, which holds that events are "meaningful coincidences" if they occur with no causal relationship, yet seem to be meaningfully related. This kind of thing might have happened before, but this time Edward was ready to learn, so the situation arose for him to make a developmental shift.

When this happened Edward felt his anger building. He was pissed off that no one understood what had happened, and that kids get bloody noses. Everyone was concerned for Jeff, and no one considered Edward's viewpoint. He managed to keep his anger in check by leaving the house and going for a drive. He had done nothing wrong to deserve his daughter's rebuke. He knew he was driving too fast, and to top it off he got a ticket for speeding. By the time he got home, everyone had left. Robin tried to reassure him, telling him that when Stacy left, Jeff wanted to know where Grandpa had gone. Edward felt sad that he had disappointed little Jeff by not being there to say good-bye, but when he told Robin that he'd gotten a speeding ticket, she was furious. The death of Edward's innocence, the death of the growing trust the others had in him, triggered great frustration and a renewal of his anger. Yet somehow, for Edward, the fact that Jeff had asked for him when he left reassured him that all the ground he had gained lately with the boy was not lost. Yet as far as Robin was concerned, the traffic ticket was proof that Edward had not really changed. Edward still thought his anger behind the wheel was justified as a way of expressing his frustration in being chastised unfairly by his daughter. His attempts to recover his innocence (which represents the death of dysfunctional behavior) with Robin failed, however, because of the ticket he held in his hand. As he had done so many times before, Edward asked himself, *What can I do?*

"You are frustrated and confused as to what you can do, just like Katy," I told him. "Let's go back to Katy, become Katy, using the Olmec Prince posture. We'll start with the Bear Spirit to calm our minds, and when I start drumming, sit with your legs crossed and your knuckles on the floor in front of you." As I started the drumming I offered, "Just think of pregnant Katy, comfortable in her routine, but then something changes. I expect her feelings could have been a lot like yours. Something unexpected happens. Jeff lands on his nose. In your frustration that no one understands, you poop on the floor. Let yourself become Katy."

After a few minutes, Edward reported, "I left and was driving too fast. I pooped on Robin. I was angry, especially at Robin. I thought she was more understanding."

As I continued drumming, I added, "Turn that around. Listen to, stalk Robin's frustration and anger when she heard about you getting a ticket, but also earlier in dealing with Jeff's bloody nose."

After a few more minutes of drumming, Edward smiled. "I wanted Robin to take care of me too, but no one cared. Katy couldn't tell me of her frustration and confusion. I guess I should be the adult, not the child."

At the next session I suggested that we again go back to Katy, Edward's spirit guide. I hoped we could bring about the death of his "childish self" and the rebirth of his "adult self." "This time I'd like to have you use the Feathered Serpent posture of standing tall with the backs of your hands resting on your hips." After a few minutes of Edward quieting his mind standing in the Bear Spirit posture, I started drumming and nodded to him to put his hands on his hips. After the fifteen minutes of drumming ended, I asked him what he had experienced.

"It was crazy. I was driving along the highway. Katy was sitting in the seat next to me. Cars were speeding everywhere, passing me on the left and the right, changing lanes and some cutting in front of me. I felt calm and in control. I had to brake several times when someone cut in front of me. I felt everyone was driving recklessly and dangerously and that I had to be calm and alert to survive. I came to the off-ramp and exited the highway. I had to turn into a heavy flow of traffic at the bottom and eased the car forward as one car slowed down and the driver motioned for me to enter. I waved to him in thanks and continued home. When I got home I parked in front of the garage and went in the back door to the back porch. My hammer was sitting on the table. I knew that Robin hadn't had the time to return it, so I took it out to the shop and went back into the house. I felt calm and in control the whole time."

"Wow, you found a very different feeling. You felt the difference between being in control and being a control freak. Good!" The experience reinforced his adult self.

GAINING OTHERS' TRUST

Edward's problem with road rage seemed to be moving toward resolution, and he had also been doing quite well with both Jeff and Lilly. Robin, on various occasions, had him hold Lilly, and it had become apparent to both of them that he had a magical touch in being able to quiet her when she was fussy. "I'm doing fine with Jeff and Lilly," he reported one day, "but something is really missing. For one thing, I'm not seeing Stacy, at least with the kids. Stacy and Robin spend their time in the kitchen while I'm with one or the other of the kids, or she just drops the kids off and leaves." He rarely saw Chuck either. He felt there was less tension between him and Stacy, though he didn't know about his son-in-law.

The day came when Robin was going to visit Stacy and wanted Edward to come along. She too thought the relationship between her husband and her daughter was going better and that it was time to bring the two families back together. Chuck was building a deck off the back of his house, and she thought Edward could help him. Though Edward was worried about working with Chuck and hesitated, he finally agreed to go along with the plan. When he got there everything seemed fine. Chuck seemed to enjoy showing Edward what he had done on the deck, and the men got busy. As the work progressed, both men seemed to be enjoying themselves. Then Edward cut one plank and went to position it on the deck, only to realize that he had cut it an inch too short. Just as Stacy came out to see how things were going, she heard her dad exclaim, "Shit!" She turned and ran back into the house, the door slamming behind her. Chuck didn't seem to think too much of it. He understood Edward's frustration. Robin came out a minute or two later and with her eyes and head motioned to Edward for them to leave. He left with his tail between his legs, but he was also angry at Stacy for being ultrasensitive.

When they got home, the telephone was ringing. Edward went directly to their bedroom and slammed the door. Robin answered the phone; it was Stacy. Apparently, Chuck was upset over Stacy's reaction and had explained to her what had happened. Stacy apologized to her mom, but the damage had been done.

In therapy Edward admitted that he wasn't angry only at Stacy, but also at himself, for saying "Shit." It was not what he wanted to do, but in that situation it just came out, and it did not feel especially inappropriate. He felt, in fact, that it was a way to show Chuck his embarrassment for making a stupid mistake in cutting the board. He realized, however, how this one outburst brought back all of Stacy's fears, fears that were so engrained that they were hard to change.

Though I believed that the goals of therapy had been met and our sessions were winding down, a couple of once-a-month sessions provided reinforcement for the changes Edward had made. He came to one session with another story about Stacy. With his new confidence in feeling the strength of trusting others, he had let down his guard with his daughter and spent some time with Jeff and Lilly while Stacy visited them. Lilly was nearly one now and was beginning to walk. Edward was encouraging her, holding his hands out to her while she took some steps toward him. He moved back little by little to see how long Lilly could stand up. She soon sat down and fell backward, bumping her head on the floor. Stacy heard Lilly's cry but did not see what had happened. Edward heard her voice rising from the other room, "What's happened now?" Edward just froze. He knew that anything he said would not be heard. It was an old pattern, and Stacy reacted automatically. Edward by then was holding Lilly to comfort her, so he took her into the other room, put her in Stacy's arms, and walked out. He felt trapped—he couldn't win with his daughter. He felt the frustration and confusion of Katy.

"Later, when Robin found me, I was just sitting in the car staring off into space. Jeff had come running into the room and told Stacy what had happened. I guess Robin knew how Stacy's words would have hurt me and told her so. Stacy went to find me to apologize, but she didn't think of looking in the garage, and she finally had to leave. Later that afternoon she phoned and apologized."

"That must have felt good. With your history of getting angry I bet you haven't heard many apologies."

"I guess you're right. I think that might've been a first."

"Stand in the Bear Spirit posture for a few minutes and feel the energy flow into you, of how good it feels to receive that apology. Feel how good it felt to not get angry and to give the other person no reason to get angry back at you. Sitting in the car, you felt hurt, and Robin knew you were hurt. By not getting angry you gave everyone the space to experience their own feelings. Jeff felt scared hearing his mother yell and did what he could to help. Robin felt your hurt, and Stacy was able to feel appropriately guilty and apologize later. It worked out well."

Edward had significantly improved his relationships with the small world of his immediate family; the goals at this stage of therapy were complete for the time being. He felt quite at peace with the family and now rarely used the Bear Spirit posture at home because he rarely felt the tension within him rise. But Edward would soon return to therapy with a new set of problems.

EXPANDING THE CIRCLE OF TRUST

Five months later, Edward phoned for an appointment.

He had been working at his current job for about two and a half years and had recently been promoted to supervisor, overseeing eight men on one production line in the plant. It was apparent that his employer liked Edward; he was dedicated and worked hard, exceeding expectations. He was proud of his promotion and took his new responsibilities to heart. He knew his wife was proud of him too. Increasing the productivity of his line became his top priority. He wanted to prove his boss's confidence in his supervisory abilities. All eight men on his line were also recognized as good workers, and there had never been any complaints about their work. The productivity of the line was satisfactory, but Edward wanted it to be exemplary. As he got to know each of the men, he observed ways in which they might improve their efficiency. He believed that this was his job. So he starting asking questions, and the men became anxious, even paranoid, when they felt him looking over their shoulders.

Even though Edward had not criticized the men's work or said anything negative about them, their suspicions about Edward's motives had been raised. One of the men finally went to the plant's human resources department to complain about this tension the men now felt in their work. Human resources contacted the plant manager about the problem, and the manager called Edward in to attempt to tactfully explain to him how his watchfulness was making the men nervous. Though Edward tried to take this in matter-of-factly, his bubble of pride burst. He was on the verge of blurting out, "I'm only doing my job. If you don't like it, I'll quit," but he managed to hold his tongue.

He returned to his work site feeling more staid. He was angry at the men, knowing that someone had complained about him, but he knew he couldn't say anything, that it would only make matters worse. Over the next few weeks Edward felt trapped, just as he had felt trapped at home when no one seemed to trust him or understand him. He also felt confused and frustrated, not unlike his spirit guide, the pregnant Katy. He couldn't talk to or watch his men, and yet that was required of his job. He found himself standing and watching from a distance. The days felt long because he felt he had nothing much to do. He spent more and more of his time cleaning up the work area, since he was appreciated for keeping his area clean and in order, but that now made him feel like a high-paid custodian. His anger was slowly building, and with it his unhappiness; he was on the verge of either quitting or exploding and losing his job.

Robin approached him one day, saying, "You seem so unhappy."

Edward told her, "I feel trapped at work. I'm not allowed to express my feelings or everyone will hate me. Everyone else can say how they feel, but I can't."

Robin didn't know what to say, so instead she reached out to hug him. He pushed her away, even though he knew he could go to her and talk with her as his partner. That was when Edward contacted me. It was time for him to get back to work.

Upon hearing what was going on in Edward's life, I recognized that the issue had to do with trust. At our session I suggested that he search for an answer to the question, "Who can I trust?" using ecstatic trance. "You couldn't trust the bullies at the bicycle rack or the bullies who took your cap," I said. "Who could you trust?"

Edward was eager to get started to see where an ecstatic trance experience would take him. After calling the spirits, I had him stand in the Bear Spirit posture with his hands on his center of harmony for five minutes to relax and quiet his mind. I then asked him to sit in the Lady of Cholula posture, sitting tall at the edge of his chair, as I began drumming.

At the end of fifteen minutes, Edward said, "I have a cousin I grew up with. We are still close. I must say he is one of the few people I trust."

"Did you ever wrestle with him?"

"We used to wrestle and punch each other all the time."

"Did you ever hurt each other?"

"Not really. Sometimes, but we didn't mean to, and we could just laugh about it."

"You trusted each other enough to wrestle and punch each other. That's bonding—doing those things that can hurt but trusting the other person enough to know that you wouldn't hurt your relationship even if you should hurt him. The bullies who took your cap—if you could have wrestled with one of them in a good-natured, playful way, you might have become friends. The two bullies were likely friends, probably wrestled with each other and could even have hurt each other and still be friends. Go back and watch those bullies."

I returned to drumming. Edward was still sitting in the Lady of Cholula posture as I prompted him further: "They are friends. They can smile and laugh together. Watch them. You feel left out and are hurt because you are alone and don't have a friend. Imagine yourself in a playful way tackling one of the boys, smiling and laughing, like you would have tackled your cousin. Feel the power of bonding when you can wrestle in a playful and fun way. You might have gained the trust of the boys who took your cap. With your weight back then you could have easily taken one of them down with a tackle . . . When you were helping Chuck while he was building the deck, was he doing it just like you would have done it?"

"Pretty much. I would have used a hammer and nails, but he had his electric screwdriver and put it together using screws."

"You didn't criticize him, you let him do it his way. You trusted him—the beginning of a healthy relationship."

"I now think screws are stronger and better than nails. They don't pull out."

"In working with Chuck, you felt your trust growing right up until Stacy interrupted. I doubt that you lost any trust with Chuck, though.

In fact, afterward he defended you to her. Nothing was wrong in your saying 'Shit!' either. Your exclamation likely showed Chuck that you cared about what you were doing, and this deepened the bond you two were creating.

"Take those thoughts with you this week. Maybe you can find others with whom you can build trust, especially at work. Think about the guys you supervise. Though you have lost their trust for now, it can be regained if you can show them you trust the work they do. With sufficient trust some occasional criticism won't hurt the relationship. Like your trust of your cousin, you are starting to trust Chuck, your two new spirit guides. Chuck has guided you to appreciate using screws rather than nails."

At our next session I suggested that Edward use the Jivaro posture to go into the underworld of his unconscious mind to find for himself a strategy for how to gain the trust of the men at work. We followed the usual ritual, starting with calling the spirits and standing in the Bear Spirit, and when I started drumming Edward reclined with his left wrist resting on his forehead. After the fifteen minutes of drumming ended, Edward related his trance experience:

"I asked the men for their ideas for making the line more efficient. I don't know why I didn't think of that before. The men seemed to appreciate me asking and seemed to trust me more."

The following week Edward reported that he tried what had come to him in trance at our last session. "One of the men came to me with an idea of placing the pallets differently at the end of the line to cut down on the traffic jam caused in the forklifts moving them." It was apparent that the men's trust in Edward was on the mend. Over the next few weeks, as he watched the men working and if they caught him watching he would give them the thumbs-up sign—that felt natural to Edward and fortified his men's trust in him.

Another problem surfaced at work. It had actually existed for a while and was reaching a critical point. There was one guy on Edward's crew, Bill, who was sometimes late for work. He had been late again, was pushing his limits, and was headed toward a suspension. This time he came to Edward with the sad story that his wife had lupus and was on dialysis. On her dialysis day he had to get the children over to a friend's house to see them off to school before work, and he cut the time too short. Edward had sympathy for Bill, but the plant's policy was clear, and he didn't have the power to change it. His tough side came out, and he told the man firmly that he would be suspended for three days if he was late one more time; one more time after that and he'd be fired. Edward had to be tough, he felt; the plant expected it. But he believed he'd lost ground in terms of the growing trust of his crew. Edward felt pulled in two directions: He was afraid that his supervisor would see him as being weak, so he had to be tough in dealing with Bill's tardiness. On the other hand, he understood Bill's problem and felt some sympathy for the man's situation. He had been in similar situations himself.

I suggested that there was another way he could have handled it. "How about if you had said to Bill, 'I understand the problem and wish there was some way I could help, but you and I both know the company's policy. The policy applies as much to me as it does to you. You are in line for being suspended for three days if you are late again.' In presenting it to Bill this way, it is not your fault if he is suspended, but the company's policy. You could give him a little moral support and still not undermine company policy. This way you are again the winner. Being understanding is being strong. You can be firm about the company policy, but you don't have to be tough on the man. You need not fear being weak, because you are being strong in showing an understanding side."

Then another member of his work group, Jack, was arrested for a DUI. Though everyone thought Jack always came to work sober, he was accused by another worker of coming in drunk. Edward was sensitive to the situation and talked to Jack, who denied drinking before work. Edward believed him, even though the rumors and accusations continued. He warned Jack about the consequences of coming to work drunk, and that other employees were talking. Then Edward told his supervisor that he had talked to Jack and did not believe the rumors were true, though he was keeping an eye on the situation. Edward's boss indicated that he appreciated him staying on top of the problem. Then another employee came to Edward with the same complaint about Jack. Edward told him that thus far he had no direct evidence that Jack had showed up for work drunk, and the man finally admitted that it was hearsay. After a few days the situation blew over. Edward felt good about the way he'd handled it. His obsession with others taking advantage of him could have been a problem in this situation—he had never liked unsubstantiated rumors, rumors that took advantage of or treated others unfairly—but he handled it tactfully.

These two incidents—the tardy employee and the one who received the DUI—taught Edward some important skills in being a supervisor. Edward had always prided himself on being on time no matter what, and he didn't drink. What these two men did was foreign to him, yet these situations taught Edward that although they had different values they could still work together, they could develop trust in one another, and they were all important members of the same team.

The ability to create trust within a wider circle of people—in this case, Edward's work environment—brought him further along on his path of awareness. This part of the journey had begun when he learned the source of the ecstatic postures—that they came from various hunter-gatherer cultures, cultures that were quite foreign to him and his experiences of life. As Edward experienced the power the postures brought him, his own consciousness began to expand. In learning how to handle the different situations that cropped up at work with the different kinds of people there, Edward was showing that he could operate with equanimity within a bigger and more diverse circle.

Then another synchronistic incident occurred that tied all this work together. The plant hired a new employee, a person from Edward's past, Jim. This was the man he had threatened who initially brought Edward to therapy through his previous employer's employee assistance program. Jim didn't work on Edward's line but on the line right next to his. Though Edward had carried resentment for this man for a while, it was now several years later. Edward had been promoted in his new job, and his life had undergone some significant changes. And so this time when he saw Jim on the other line for the first time, he walked up to him and gave him a playful shove with a big smile of greeting on his face. When the man turned to see who had pushed him, Edward's smile disarmed him.

"He didn't know what to think," Edward told me, laughing. I was pleased to hear this; this was the very same imagery I had used with Edward in facing his long-ago nemesis, the junior high bullies, but it was the first time he had had a chance to actually try this strategy. He was excited to see how effective it was and how spontaneous he felt in playfully shoving the guy and experiencing the bonding that resulted. Jim gave him a big smile back, and for the rest of the week and until Edward came in to see me the next time, both men couldn't help but smile whenever they saw each other. Finally Edward was feeling the power of trust and bonding. This newfound power caused the death of his anger. The dysfunctional belief that others were out to take advantage of him and that they shouldn't be allowed to "get away with it" was now dead. Innocence had been reborn in Edward—the essence of soul retrieval—and it had him grinning from ear to ear.

The goals of therapy had been met; a couple of once-a-month sessions provided additional reinforcement for the changes in Edward's life. In becoming aware of the origin of his explosive temper, he no longer needed to get angry to protect himself and his self-image. As a result, he found a new closeness and intimacy with his family and gained respect from his wider circle of coworkers. He discovered that he could trust others, and that this trust greatly improved all his relationships. He was finding that he didn't have to stand alone against the world to survive, and that he and others could bond and face this world together, thus increasing their strength and effectiveness. In the course of this journey he had grown beyond his old self-centered world and found he could maintain his equanimity in an expanded new world of people with different values and beliefs. He had learned to trust and respect his animal spirit guides, and the different cultures that the ecstatic postures came from, which added yet another dimension to his appreciation of the wider world around him.

At one of our last sessions I told Edward about the ecstatic trance group that meets about once a month to use ecstatic trance postures for continued personal and spiritual growth, and I suggested that he might want to join the group, telling him that there was no charge for being in it. He was eager to join. In the group his world continued to expand. Along with calling the spirits of each direction, smudging with herbal smoke is one more element of ecstatic trance that he had not experienced, and he was learning to value its cleansing effect. He was discovering the interdependence of all that is of the Earth and was valuing more highly what the Earth around him had to offer. One concrete result was that he, like others in the group, planted a garden and was proud of it.

5

Balancing Freedom
and Responsibility

A Case Study of
Infidelity and Feeling Empty

*Coyote sings the stories of healing, the stories of forgiveness
and reconciliation, the stories of transformation.*

LEWIS MEHL-MADRONA

Jen, thirty six, offered her story in our first session. It was obvious that she saw some value in having an extramarital affair—the good feelings of intimacy with another person—yet she was also experiencing painful feelings of guilt and failure in maintaining her value of fidelity. Her extramarital affair greatly shocked her and began to make her look at her life differently. Sometimes people who have affairs find justifications for why they do so and do nothing to change the way they look at life. Jen dealt with her situation by letting it bring her to therapy—a positive step.

Her affair was a sign of her discontent, of her feeling empty and wanting more closeness and intimacy in her life. Jen had found someone who could empathize with her loneliness and pain, thus filling the void. She had let the affair go on for too long, whether it was out of a need to thank her lover for being there for her or simply because her growing intimacy with him felt so good that she couldn't stop herself,

143

or both. In any case, she was upset and shocked at herself for what she was doing in her struggle to end the affair. Jen believed that if she could end it she would never do it again, so she entered therapy as a precautionary measure, as a way of forcing herself to make her guilt known, at least as much as the privacy and confidentiality of a psychologist's office could offer. The therapy room is a secular confessional. Whether consciously or unconsciously, Jen believed that by "confessing" in this way it would prevent her from sliding back into yet another affair.

A NEED FOR INTIMACY

The word that Jen used to describe what was missing in her marriage was *intimacy*. She felt empty. If I had supported her feelings of emptiness, some rapport between us might have been gained, but then I would have been offering her emotional support for having an affair. By instead offering a counternarrative in the form of a story called "The History of the Family," I was able to support her need for intimacy but also offer her an alternative way to fulfilling that need.

"Some years ago in some magazine I read an article on the history of the family," I told her. "The article suggested that most likely your grandparents or great-grandparents were farmers. The husband worked hard in the fields all day, while his wife cared for the children and preserved the food. He'd come in at night and crash. There really wasn't much of what we call intimacy. This family was a child-rearing economic unit. It was the way to survive. For intimacy, the wife might visit with a group of women, likely relatives, and over the quilting frame they would talk about their feelings. The husband might go to the general store on Saturday morning and talk with the other men around the potbelly stove.

"But then things changed. Along came the Industrial Revolution, and this couple moved to the city. The husband went to work in a factory, came home at night, and would crash. The wife took care of the children and the house. Once again, intimacy was missing. But this time there was no opportunity for intimacy between the women of the urban neighborhood like there had been before in a country setting where women would get together to quilt and visit. At this point the wife began to expect her husband to fulfill all her needs, including her need for intimacy. She began to feel empty. This situation brought about the invention of psychology. Though I think it is important to teach men the meaning of intimacy, many of them have a difficult time learning it. Their way is to do, not feel."

With this story I hoped to ignite the wisdom and intuition within Jen, to provide her with a new understanding of the meaning of intimacy.

Jen's fear about having another extramarital affair was most likely a fear of being caught and losing her husband, Bruce. These fears couldn't be discounted, but the fear she expressed when she first came to me was the fear of losing her integrity, as she had betrayed her marriage. This fear expressed her feelings of guilt over the affair. Therapeutically, I repeatedly brought her back to this feeling of guilt and had her focus on this guilt and talk about it. It expanded into the fear of, "What will people think?" and the fear of disappointing her parents.

Her fears were much more personalized—for example, a fear of losing her integrity rather than of "What will others think?"—which seemed healthy. We didn't talk much about her fear of being caught and losing Bruce. In looking back at these first couple of sessions, my thinking was that Jen either felt she deserved to lose her husband, or she somehow had faith in him that he wouldn't reject her even if he knew about her affair. But beyond these two possibilities, she believed that Bruce's inability to express intimacy made him blind to her needs. In fact, she believed he didn't have enough sensitivity to recognize or even think that she was capable of having an affair.

By our third session I realized that Jen's vivid description of her fears suggested that she was a good candidate for ecstatic trance, that her trance experiences would likely be very vivid. The ability to vividly be able to describe feelings is an activity of the right brain and a characteristic of trance.

I wanted Jen to connect directly to her feelings, so instead of using the Lady of Cholula posture to ask a question as I normally would when first starting out in ecstatic trance therapy, we would use the Jivaro

Underworld posture to take her into her unconscious. There would be plenty of opportunities to use the Lady of Cholula posture later.

I explained that we would start out using a simple technique to relax the body, quiet the mind, and find inner peace and strength: "Stand with your hand resting on your abdomen, which is your center of harmony, so that you can feel your abdomen rise and fall as you breathe from your diaphragm. With each breath inhale a sense of calm strength, and as you exhale let that calm strength flow throughout your body." I demonstrated the Bear Spirit posture, though I did not call it that in this first session with the postures.

"Continue to follow your breathing like this for a few minutes until I start the recorded drumming, and then lie down on the couch with your left wrist resting on your forehead, like this." I demonstrated the Jivaro posture by lying back in my recliner with the back of my left hand resting on my forehead. I told her, "This posture is used for journeying into the underworld of your unconscious mind. The drumming stimulates your nervous system and helps you go into a state of trance for this journey. As you go into trance, carry with you your fear of what other people may think, the fear of disappointing your parents, and see where this trance experience takes you."

Jen commented that she had seen in movies where the psychoanalyst had the client lie on the couch for journeying into the unconscious mind.

After a few minutes in the Bear Spirit posture I started the drumming recording, and we both took the Jivaro posture. She quickly went into a deep trance, and her increased rate of breathing indicated that her experience was causing her some anxiety. At the end of the fifteen minutes of drumming, I asked her about what she had experienced.

"I found myself in a cheap motel room; it smelled smoky. When I looked out the window I could see the cars going by on the street. I saw Bruce's car go by. Then I saw his car again and again, several of them in a row, all going by. I heard the phone buzzing on the hook, like someone might have tapped the room and could hear what was going on inside my head. I could hear a scraping sound on the wall from the room next door. I was terrified. It was a disgusting B movie set. I was scared; I didn't want to be there. It's not where my affair happened, but it could have been. In my trance I don't think anyone else was there with me. Ben [the man with whom she had had the affair] wasn't there. I was alone in this very derelict place. It looked filthy and disgusting. Then the scene changed, and I saw this laughing, inflated clown, sort of like Ronald McDonald, but more red and white than yellow. It was moving, bending back and forth at the waist, bowing and laughing a mocking laugh, a laugh I hated. I wanted to run and hide."

"What did you feel?"

"Fear. Guilt. Disgust. I couldn't stand the clown. He was laughing at me."

"What part of you is laughing in a mocking, disgusting way?"

She didn't answer. We both knew the answer. We sat silently for a few minutes. Silence added to her ownership of her feelings that had been so effectively revealed by this trance experience. It was the world and herself, not her family or Bruce, who was mocking her. She sat with her blue eyes staring blankly and her straight blond hair hanging inertly around her narrow face and over her shoulders. The only movement was the rhythmic rising and falling of her abdomen.

Compared to some clients who blame others or find excuses for having an affair, Jen's fear was at a deeper level, a more abstract fear. Jen was a bright and sensitive woman with high integrity, and this fear had been with her from the beginning. She didn't need to articulate it.

The disgust and humiliation Jen had experienced in the previous session, in which she was mocked by the inflated clown, was illuminating, so in the next session I suggested we take that experience further by going back in time to an earlier experience of humiliation. Again, the Jivaro posture was the most effective way to do that. We repeated the same induction ritual of following her breathing while standing in the Bear Spirit posture, and then reclining in the Jivaro posture. I suggested that as she went into trance she take her feelings of humiliation and disgust back through time to an earlier time when she felt humiliated and disgusted. As before, I could feel and experience, while also in trance, the progress of her trance experience in the change in the depth and rate of her breathing.

At the end of the fifteen minutes of drumming I asked her to report on her experience. She said that as she proceeded back through the years, she came to a time in her early adolescence, a time when she was feeling her newly flowing hormones, yet feeling clumsy and awkward. "I felt so embarrassed. Lucy told me what she had heard. Lucy was my best friend. She told me what the boys were talking about. One asked her if I really lap danced. They were all saying that I lap danced with Jeremy. The problem was that I did it on a dare and thought he would like it. I had a crush on him. I think he did like it, but afterward I couldn't face him. When he saw me he just smiled, and the other kids laughed. I never did live that down. It was so bad for a while that I didn't go to school for a week, and only when the school threatened to fine my family did I go back. At that point it was only a few days until the end of the school year."

I wasn't sure I knew what she meant by lap dancing, but I could imagine it well enough that I didn't feel a need to ask. The fear of going back to school, the fear of facing those who knew or who might find out, the humiliation and the self-disgust were intense, more than the fear of the loss of her integrity. A loss of integrity is too cerebral. Humiliation is much more in the gut.

"Wow, how humiliating. I'm impressed that you could go back to your school years."

"Oh, I just hid in my books, sat in the back of the room, and snuck in and out of classes. One teacher who liked me let me hang out in her room during lunch. Actually, I remember that my grades were pretty good that year because I hid in the books."

TAKING A CLOSER LOOK AT GUILT

Jen's fear and guilt were evidently part of the same package. Her experience of being in a grungy hotel and seeing the laughing, inflated clown were images of both. At our next session she described a dream she had had the previous week:

"I was sitting in the interrogation box in a courtroom. The judge was wearing a black robe, but his face was painted like the clown I told you about last week. He was laughing, same as the clown. A lawyer in a suit, but also with a clown head, was standing in front of the box laughing that mocking laugh. I woke up. I knew I was guilty."

Jen hated herself and felt terrorized by her guilt and told me she was doing everything she could do to avoid seeing Ben. "When he makes his deliveries he comes into the office to leave his invoice. I generally can see his truck drive up. I give him about ten minutes and then find an excuse to leave the office. But one day last week I missed seeing the truck and was there when he came in. He asked where I had been. I didn't know what to say, I just stammered and sputtered. My heart was racing. I feel like I'm going crazy."

I didn't think I needed to say anything. It was time for Jen to experience her guilt, to feel her feelings of going crazy. My silence allowed her to own these feelings.

At the next session Jen reported that her four-year-old daughter, Crissy, had asked her, "What's wrong, Mommy?" Jen had no idea how Crissy knew something was wrong with her, but she did. The intuition of young children is amazing. Crissy's question occurred on a morning after Jen had once again seen Ben at the office. Jen was quick to reply, "Oh nothing, I just had a hard day at work yesterday," and she gave Crissy a big hug, but that afternoon when Jen came into my office she was in tears.

Again there was not a great need for me to say anything. I did explain how children are very much more in touch with their feelings than adults are, and that I didn't know specifically what Crissy was experiencing, whether it was a feeling that Jen was just preoccupied or if it was Jen's guilty feelings. But in either case, Crissy knew something was off with her mom. Did Bruce know something was wrong? The ability of adults, especially men, to intuit others' feelings is not nearly as great as that of children. Bruce likely was either blind to his own intuition or dismissed any suspicions by assuming that Jen had had a hard day or that something was bothering her that she didn't want to talk about. He most likely did not experience Jen's emotional state as threatening, like a young child would.

Jen's guilty feelings were affecting her daughter, and this made her self-loathing more pronounced. In time she might discover other issues that involved guilt, but Crissy was the most important person in Jen's life. Being a mother was her ultimate concern, and her daughter's ability to sense that something was wrong with her was proof of the close bond between mother and daughter.

I offered, "What is healthy about this situation is that Crissy is able to read you, and that means that there is a healthy bond between the two of you." Though I didn't want to take away from Jen's experience of guilt, it was important to begin to lay the groundwork in therapy of focusing on the positive rather than the negative. It was apparent that Jen had difficulty forming lasting, healthy bonds with adult men, and recognizing her bond with her daughter was a beginning for Jen to learn how to bond with others. In the terminology of Michael Yapko, I was able to deamplify Jen's emotional distance and amplify bonding.[1] It was more important to focus on the positive, on her ability to bond with Crissy, than to focus on the negative, the emotional distance she experiences with others that causes her to feel empty in life.

NEEDING TO BE NEEDED

At our next session, another, deeper level of guilt came to the surface. I was wondering what had attracted Jen to her husband, Bruce, in the first place. In earlier sessions she had mentioned that Bruce was reliable, a good person, and that she was needy and wanted the respect that marriage could bring. When she first met Bruce he was just out of school. "Partying was more important than working. He was out of work and looking for a job. He would hold a job for a few weeks but would decide he didn't like it and quit. But I fell in love with him. Somehow I thought I could make him a better person." Bruce regarded Jen as the "together" one, the one who could take care of things. She was responsible. She had a job and stuck with it. "We had been married for about five years, and I wanted a baby, and Bruce knew it. He had held a job for about six months and seemed restless. I told him I wanted a baby, but I needed the assurance that he was going to have steady work and be responsible. Though he had not seemed enthusiastic about having children, when I brought up wanting a baby it did something to him. I think he started to think about what it would mean to be a father. He was working in a local food-processing plant that was unionized, one of the higher-paying places in the area. He came home one night and announced that he had been promoted to lead man on his line. He was pleased with himself. From then on, somehow his attitude changed. He started coming home every night and stopped going to the bar with his friends. Somehow a weight was lifted off my shoulders. I got pregnant, and Crissy was born. I always knew that Bruce was smart. About two years ago, a position in the sales department opened up. He applied for it and got it. His income doubled, and he has since won awards for being one of the best salesmen. He can talk enthusiastically about his successes at work, but he doesn't talk about us. I feel so empty. His life is his work. He doesn't need me."

"Bruce doesn't need you. Ben needs you more. You feel so empty, and Bruce is not filling that emptiness." Jen's breathing changed. I could see she was becoming anxious, so I kept to the counternarrative, not giving her a chance to use this reasoning as a justification. "You feel good when someone needs you, when you can rescue them, but once they get on their feet you abandon them for someone else whom you can rescue." I didn't have to make Jen feel guiltier about the affair, but now her guilt was about something deeper, a personality trait: her need to be needed. She could have used her need to be needed as a justification for the affair, but in articulating the fact that she abandons people once they get on their feet, a deeper feeling of guilt was triggered.

I suggested that we again go into the underworld of her unconscious mind after we first used the Bear Spirit posture of standing with our hands on our center of harmony to increase her sense of quiet strength and inner peace. She then lay back on the couch with the wrist of her left hand resting on her forehead as I turned on the drumming and lay back in a similar position in my recliner. At the end of the fifteen minutes, Jen related her experience:

"I found myself sitting on the floor, pulling off my daddy's work boots. When he came home from work he would plop down on his recliner, exhausted. He worked in construction. His boots smelled dusty. He helped me get his boots off by pushing with one foot on the heel of the boot that I was trying to pull off. I set the boots by the door as I ran to get his slippers. He reached down and scratched me on the head and smiled as I put on his slippers. I don't remember when I started doing this. I think maybe Mom did it when I was smaller. I think I did this for him until I left home and got married."

Jen continued her narrative: "I remember doing a lot around the house. My room was always especially neat compared to the rooms of my friends. Looking back, I think I enjoyed putting away my things as much as I enjoyed playing with them. I remember thinking how hard Mom and Dad worked, Mom in keeping the house together and cooking the meals. I can still see Mom wiping her forehead with her sleeve as she would plop in her recliner next to Daddy's, but soon she would jump up again to get busy doing something else. I needed to help her. She seemed tired, but I don't remember her complaining."

As Jen described her early experiences, she included more and more details, details that triggered even deeper feelings. In this way she was exceptional in the depth of her ecstatic experiences.

Obsessing came naturally to Jen. She had become very worried about Crissy because her daughter had noticed that something was wrong with her. Her fear and guilt perpetuated her obsessive worrying. All three feelings are just different aspects of a person's personality pattern, with its automatic cognitive, somatic, emotional, and behavioral responses to life situations.

With Jen's understanding of her need to be needed—something she saw nothing wrong with—I thought it was time for her to realize how and why this wasn't working for her. It was time to use the Lady of Cholula posture, asking the question, "What happens when I am not needed?"

I had her sit tall on the edge of her chair, clasping her left knee with her left hand and resting her right hand on top of her right thigh, as I demonstrated the position to her. I asked her what she thought this posture expressed. Her answer was quite accurate. She said that she felt like she was waiting alertly for the answer to her question. After having her find quiet strength in standing with her hands on her center of harmony, I turned on the drumming, and she sat in this posture while I sat in the same posture. Observing her breathing, I saw her anxiety building. After the fifteen minutes of drumming ended, Jen related her experience:

"What came to me was a dream I had a couple of nights ago. I was planning to tell you this dream when I came to the session, but it was so vivid in trance, like I was reliving it. I was surfing the Internet and somehow a bunch of pornography appeared on the screen. I couldn't get back to what I was searching for. I tried the back button, and all I got was more pornography. I tried to go back to a search engine, but more and more pornography popped up. I took my hands off the keyboard and mouse, but still more pornography came up. I was in a panic; I didn't want anyone to find out that I was into porn. I tried to shut the computer down, but it wouldn't shut down. I unplugged it, but even that didn't work. I've heard that people who know what they're doing can somehow find the websites I have searched in the past. I was frantic. I didn't want anyone to know I was looking at porn. The dream seemed to go on forever, repeating again and again until finally the alarm went off. I woke up exhausted. I have never gone to a porn site in my life."

I responded, "When you feel not needed, you will likely do something that makes you feel guilty, something you don't have any control over. You know what you are doing is wrong, but you feel the action is out of your control."

Jen left the session feeling that she had the strength to stick to her commitment to avoid Ben when he made deliveries at her office. Yet on the rare occasion that she did see him she would panic, and this panic reinforced her recognition that she needed to avoid him. At the next session we began to explore how she saw Ben.

"He has never made a real commitment to a woman in his life."

"So maybe you could rescue him if he could make a commitment to you. So where does that leave the two of you? If he makes a commitment to you, then you won't need him, and anyway you are really not ready to make a commitment to him. If he makes a commitment to you and you reject it, it will make it harder for him to make any commitment in the future. He will trust women even less. If he has never made a commitment to a woman, then you could say that he uses women and then abandons them. You are using him, too, to fill your own need to rescue."

"I hadn't thought of it that way."

"No one thinks much about it when they get into such situations. But when you allow yourself to think about it, you begin to find the strength to do the right thing." This way of thinking gave Jen the additional support she needed to help her deal with her anxiety. And by discovering the absurdity of her need to rescue Ben, she found the wisdom she needed to help her more effectively deal with him.

That Ben made his deliveries every other day, and that on those days Jen spent time avoiding him, kept her torment alive. She was beginning to realize that she would someday need to stop running away from him. Just picking up and leaving the office whenever he came in was becoming a nuisance and interfered with her work. She knew she needed to deal with Ben in an appropriate and direct way. By telling him the affair was over she hoped that she would get his cooperation. And when she did tell him, she was pleased that he was honorable enough to tell her that he accepted her decision. Still, the next time he made a delivery, he looked at Jen in a sad and longing way, which set off Jen's inner turmoil such that she was distracted for the rest of the afternoon. The next day, when Ben didn't come to the office, she felt her strength return and made a commitment to not let his hangdog look bother her. This was much easier said than done, however, because "the next day when he did come in I was once again a mess for the rest of the afternoon."

Jen's need to rescue was easily hooked by the forlorn looks Ben was shooting in her direction. She felt hopeless about ending the affair, but she was determined to try. Jen knew Ben's schedule after work and knew where he would be. One day she phoned Bruce to tell him she would be home a little late because of some extra work she had to do. She left not sure of what she was going to say to Ben. When she got to the truck stop, she saw his truck. Her heart was racing when she entered the restaurant and saw him across the room. She knew what was going to happen. He saw her, and she turned and left. He followed her out as they walked toward his truck. What she knew was going to happen did. The chain of willpower was broken.

"You feel he needs you sexually. Your need to be needed is fulfilled by giving him what he needs, and that's exciting. You too are excited by him sexually, yet you are disgusted with yourself at the same time. You just don't know what to do. You can't let go of him, you can't hurt him, you can't simply forget about him, about someone who excites you so. You're a mess. It sounds like you need a vacation from this mess."

Jen had to agree with me. "Bruce has been asking if we can take a vacation and get away to his folks' hunting camp." She seemed ready to change subjects to get away from the pain of how Ben excited her.

"Can you get away?"

"I told Bruce that I'm behind on my work and can't get away now."

"But is there some way you can get away?"

"I guess so. I'm not that far behind, and I'm not the only person in the office."

"It sounds like you are hesitant to be alone with Bruce and Crissy for a few days, maybe even afraid."

"Uh-huh. I don't know any more what to say to Bruce, what to talk about."

"How about if you arrange some vacation time. Tell Bruce. We can talk about what you can talk about with Bruce at the next session. For the time being, go back to avoiding Ben by leaving the office when you see him driving up."

ENCOUNTER WITH THE WOLF

At our next session I told Jen I thought she needed a spirit guide to help her understand her need to be needed. "You are a rescuer, a seeing-eye dog whose whole life is to serve others. Bruce has found himself in his work. He's proud of what he has accomplished in his salesmanship and has found fulfillment in himself, and you feel he doesn't need you. He doesn't need a seeing-eye dog to show him the way. What's the alternative? It's for you too to find fulfillment in yourself.

"I'd like you to sit at the edge of your chair clasping your knees, sitting in anticipation of an answer. Let's first start by standing tall for the next few minutes with our hands at our center of harmony, feeling the healing and strengthening energy entering us and quieting our minds. When I start the drumming, sit and clasp your knees in anticipation of an answer to how you can find fulfillment in yourself." After I started the recorded drumming, I sat in the same posture. Following our fifteen-minute trance session, Jen recalled her experience, in which it was evident that she had picked up on my visual cue:

"I first thought of the many different breeds of dogs. I realized that they were all domesticated and bred to serve humans in different ways. I saw the dog I had as a child, waiting at the window watching for the school bus to stop in front of our house, just waiting for me to get home. I loved our dog, and she loved me. I couldn't think of a dog that was independent, who had a life of her own, until I thought of where all these breeds of dogs came from: from the wolf. In the trance, as a wolf, I had the independence, the responsibility of taking care of myself and my pups. I had a choice of a male wolf mate, one that would help provide food for our pups. We worked together and with the larger pack."

I ended the session with this suggested direction for Jen: "Try to spend some time with your spirit guide, the wolf. Feel her strength and independence, of sharing responsibility with your mate to provide, care for, and teach your pups."

When Jen arrived for our next session I suggested we try a new posture, the Olmec Prince, to get inside the experience of being her spirit guide, the wolf. I demonstrated the posture: sitting on the floor with your legs crossed and the knuckles of your fingers resting on the floor in front of you. She quickly agreed that the position of the knuckles on the floor felt like forepaws—"Like the front legs of the wolf, your powerfully independent spirit guide," I added.

We started out as usual in the Bear Spirit posture, and as I started the drumming recording we both assumed the posture of the Olmec Prince. Following the fifteen-minute session with the posture she related her experience:

"I found myself sitting in front of our den, and the wolf pups were crawling all over me. I knew how to be a good mother, nursing the pups and watching over them so they didn't wander off. Their father brought home some meat that we chewed up and regurgitated and fed to the pups. My whole life was being a mother to the pups. I was completely focused on them and never away from our den. After a while I was able to take the pups out and begin to show them how to hunt. I was a responsible mother wolf, and my partner helped."

I added, "With Bruce's help as your partner, you can be a responsible mother to Crissy in showing her how to live."

At our session the following week we decided to take this wolf experience to an even deeper level using the Feathered Serpent posture. Jen related the following:

"I first saw my wolf self and my partner watching over our pups. Then they became me and Bruce watching Crissy playing in the creek. She enjoys so much playing in the water with her bucket and shovel, digging and building dams to make pools of water and playing in the pools. She loves being outdoors, watching the occasional fish, salamanders, and water insects. There is so much about nature for her to experience. Bruce grew up spending a lot of time at his family's hunting camp. He knows every rock and tree around the camp and enjoys teaching her about all those things when we go there. We sit on the porch and see an occasional deer, squirrels, and many different birds. We put up a suet feeder, and she is learning about the birds that come to the feeder, woodpeckers, titmice, and others. I was a city girl until I was a teenager and we moved to the country. I've learned so much from him about nature."

This experience reminded Jen of how much she enjoyed their visits to the cabin. She opened up and wanted to tell me all about it. "It's a rustic cabin. Three rooms, a large living room with three single beds along the wall, with a sink, wood-burning stove, and refrigerator at one end. The other two rooms are small bedrooms, and we use an outhouse out back. There's a gas-powered generator out in the shed to run the water pump, the lights, and the refrigerator. That's sort of noisy, but we're used to it. Anyway, there is a stream not far from the cabin that we can hear, too. I love it when it rains on the tin roof." She laughed quietly. "I hadn't thought about it, the sounds we hear. I've thought about the sounds of the cabin, as opposed to the television that is always on at home . . .

"Bruce likes to stay busy even when we're out there. He wants to paint the tin roof on this trip. But he also likes to just sit on the porch and watch Crissy. He'll read and probably take one of his Civil War novels. I'll take my knitting, and a book, too.

"How about food? What do you eat?"

"We have a tradition that when we first get there Bruce starts the generator, then lights the stove, puts on a kettle, and warms up a large can of baked beans. We don't eat fancy there. We'll take bread and lunch meat. Probably macaroni and cheese, stuff like that. We'll probably go to the store, which is about six miles away, once during the week, to get milk, and we'll probably get a pizza."

"You were worried about what you would talk about. You sound really excited and that talking with Bruce is not a concern, that there is so much to do and enjoy there." I could see that in recalling her experiences at the cabin Jen was still in a state of trance, so I continued. "I assume there is some comfortable furniture inside the cabin—why don't you picture yourself sitting on the couch watching Bruce busying himself with lighting the stove and getting the baked beans ready. Relax. Feel comfortable. Appreciate Bruce. Feel the warmth inside of you while watching Bruce. Once Bruce has the beans heated, he comes over and sits next to you on the couch. Rest your head on his shoulder. Nothing needs to be said. Just feel good. If you feel like it, say what comes to your mind about how good it feels to be there. Maybe talk about the sounds and smells, the sounds of the birds and creek and the scent of the burning wood and the beans heating, or the outdoorsy smells of the woods; the feeling of having Bruce right next to you. Or talk about what Crissy is doing . . .

"During these next few days before you go on your vacation, think about these things. Think about going for a walk together holding hands. Think about after Crissy goes to sleep at night, what might happen between you and Bruce. Think about your usual camping routine, but also think about what you might do differently that you would enjoy and find exciting. Think about your time with him in bed. You might like to share your thoughts with Bruce, or you might just surprise him. Take these thoughts with you, and let them grow. With new possibilities growing within you, feel the excitement of going to the camp grow."

REVEALING THE POSTURES

By now Jen had experienced all five postures I use in therapy, so it was time to tell her about Felicitas Goodman and the origins of the postures that we'd been using. In giving her this background information I showed her the pictures of these postures and talked about where each one came from. I explained that using this sequence of postures in healing work is often called *soul retrieval,* the task of retrieving some part of the self and your innocence that has been lost over the years.

Jen was an open-minded person who thought of herself as a new age person and practiced yoga regularly, so this story of the postures and the spirit guides fit well with her way of life.

After returning from her vacation at the cabin, Jen told me she'd had an enjoyable trip, better than she thought it would be. "Crissy and especially Bruce thought the trip was great. I did what you suggested. I thought about our time together in bed and what we could do before we left on the trip. We had a great time, especially Bruce. He was surprised and excited about our lovemaking. There's nothing wrong with Bruce."

Yet Ben was still on Jen's mind. "Everything Bruce and I did fit together fine, but with Ben it's different—more exciting, newer, freer. I don't know why I keep thinking the word *free* except that we have no expectations of each other, no responsibilities. I don't have to do anything special for him, and I don't expect anything from him. With Bruce there are all kinds of expectations and responsibilities because of our life together. At the cabin I sometimes did what Ben and I have done in our lovemaking. I felt a little guilty about it, but it made Bruce happy, and he wasn't the wiser.

"I'd watch Bruce and Crissy together and feel happy for them and for us. I wondered how Crissy and Ben would get along. I know that it wouldn't be the same as with her father. Step relationships are often painful, but I would like to share that part of my life with Ben. Crissy is part of me, and I want Ben to know that part of me. But Crissy is part of Bruce, and Ben would see that. That thought is painful, but I still sometimes think of sharing all of me with Ben."

I let Jen ramble on. She had been doing a lot of thinking and needed to hear her own thoughts. Finally it was my turn to speak.

"You've tried to ignore Ben for a few weeks, and you were successful when you were too busy to think about him. On your vacation you had a lot of time to think, so he was still alive inside of you. Bruce and Crissy are so much a part of you, but Ben is so much part of you in a different way. Ben is exciting. You feel free with Ben because you don't have responsibilities together. With Bruce and Crissy, the responsibilities are heavy; they are work."

Jen jumped in with "responsibilities are what makes life, marriage, and a family work. The freedom of an affair is exciting, but it's irresponsible; it takes away from the family, from what life is really all about."

"You know this, yet it's still hard to let go of the excitement and freedom of an affair."

"Yeah, it's hard." I sensed that Jen felt it was liberating to talk about the affair, and in a way that freed her from the guilt she had been beating herself up with.

At our next session I thought it would be useful to return to the Jivaro Underworld posture to carry her thinking about the irresponsibility of having Ben in her life into her unconscious mind. We had last used the Olmec Prince posture when she became the nurturing she-wolf. The Olmec Prince is a metamorphosis posture and can bring about a change not unlike what happens in using the Feathered Serpent in providing a death and rebirth experience.

After going through our usual induction ritual and then assuming the Jivaro posture for a full fifteen minutes of drumming, Jen related the following:

"When I was fourteen, after we moved to the country, I had a goat for a 4-H project. I milked her in the morning and at night and made cheese with the milk. In my trance I was milking the goat but crying because I knew my friends were having a party and I was going to miss it. While I was crying I buried my face in the flank of the goat, and it felt so soft and warm. In reality I had the goat for about six months and loved it, but I sold it at an auction soon after school started in the fall because it took up so much time. Between school and the goat I didn't have any time for my friends. The goat's name was Strawberry. She was an Alpine and a very good milker."

I could hear her love for her goat in her voice. "You were close to Strawberry. I bet it was hard for you to sell her, but your friends were important too. It was a hard decision, but it wasn't a hard decision. You knew what you had to do."

"I could have let her dry up, but milking her was much of why I loved her."

"It's pretty obvious, but what in your life are you struggling with to give up like you gave up Strawberry?"

"Ben."

"Or your family."

"Oh, I could never give up my family!"

"Like you couldn't give up your friends, you couldn't give up your family. As important as Strawberry was to you, your friends were more important. It really hurts to give up Strawberry, just like it hurts to give up Ben. In looking back to Strawberry and your friends, did you make the right decision?"

"Yeah, my friends are still my friends. They are still important to me. I don't know what ever happened to Strawberry . . . "

"But you've never forgotten Strawberry. I can still hear the love for her in your voice. You'll never forget Ben, either. Tell me about selling Strawberry, about your feelings."

"I cried for a few days. I stayed away from my friends. I didn't want them to see me crying, and I even hated them some for making me sell Strawberry, though they really didn't make me sell her."

"Let me throw in another word to see how it fits. You felt very *guilty* about selling Strawberry, and you needed to blame your friends for making you feel guilty in order to take away some of the pain of your guilt. You knew that Strawberry loved you and depended on you too. You felt guilty for abandoning her, even though she may have ended up in a loving home."

"I don't know. I tried to find a home for her. As a last resort I took her to the auction, and there you have no idea where she is going. Goats are often bought at an auction for meat. I always hoped she didn't go for meat. She had papers, and the good price I got made me think that she went to someone who was going to milk her."

"It was so hard to sell Strawberry. You eventually forgave your friends."

"That didn't take too long. My mother had a surprise birthday party for me the next weekend, and all my friends were there."

"You never forgot Strawberry. You'll never forget Ben. Your family will be there for you, but something about Ben will always be part of you."

With this experience Jen now had three animal spirit guides: the seeing-eye dog, the wolf, and Strawberry the goat. I told her that the power of spirit guides lies in their ability to help a person change. "Similarly, in using ecstatic trance we also call the spirits of the directions. Calling the spirits of each direction, East, South, West, North, the Universe, and Mother Earth, is part of our ecstatic trance ritual. We call the spirits before we use the Bear Spirit posture that provides us with a quiet, peaceful internal strength we need to go into trance." I told her that now I would do the drumming myself rather than using a recording. We had not yet incorporated the smudging into our ritual, but I knew that if at some point she joined our monthly ecstatic trance group she would learn about that aspect of the induction ritual. Being open to alternative and new age methods, calling the spirits fit well with her lifestyle, and probably smudging would have too.

"There is something else you can learn from Strawberry. I would like you to become Strawberry and experience the first few times she stood on the milk stand. We will use the Olmec Prince posture, where you sit on the floor with your knuckles resting on the floor in front of you."

After the experience, Jen told me about becoming Strawberry: "Jen led me up to the milk stand. She had a bowl of grain for me and held it in front of me. I stepped up on the stand, and she held the bowl on the other side of where I was to put my head. I stuck my head through, and she locked my head between two pieces of wood, but I had the grain to eat. When she put her hands on my udder and rubbed it I jumped at first, but then it felt good. When she grabbed and pulled on one of my teats, I started dancing. I didn't know what was going on, but as she pulled and the milk squirted out, I felt some relief of the pressure of the milk in my udder. I soon stopped dancing, and it felt good. Jen was gentle, and I trusted her. She always fed me and took care of me. When she was done, she released my head and let me go back to the barn."

"Good. How long did it take for her to learn the routine of being milked?"

"Only two or three times. She was a quick learner, and after that she seemed to look forward to being milked."

I responded, "At first she was confused and maybe a little frightened. Hopefully the new owner was as gentle and understanding as you. But it takes being gentle and patient with yourself to learn something new in life, of learning to be the good mother and good wife, something you are learning as a result of your experience in having an extramarital affair. Your feelings have led you on a journey of self-discovery that has opened new doors to how you feel and experience life."

LETTING GO

With Jen's shape-shifting goat experience, I felt that she was ready to give up her obsession with Ben. My role was to provide her with emotional support over the next few sessions as the drama unfolded.

Jen thought about Ben a lot and saw him several days a week when he came into the office. She made a point to be friendly around him, but no friendlier than she would with any other vendor. She was not seductively friendly or encouraging. Though she left open the possibility that there might be a day when she might confront him by telling him she was ending the affair, she put off that day with her reserved behavior and subdued feelings. She felt withdrawn from everything, even at home with Bruce and Crissy, but that was okay. Bruce and Crissy seemed to enjoy the quiet evenings at home and their time together. Bruce was a good father.

One day Ben came into Jen's office and commented that he had not seen her lately at the Hilltop. The Hilltop was a popular bar-restaurant known for its good sandwiches; it was the place where she and Ben used to meet. Jen replied, "I know. I haven't felt like going anywhere. I've been feeling tired, just too busy." As Ben was leaving, he touched Jen's hand. Beneath her somber exterior her heart was racing.

Another time when he came in, Jen was the only one in the office. This time he was more direct: "When are you going to come by the Hilltop again? I miss you."

Jen put off his question with the excuse, "Maybe next week. I may have more time then. Just too many things going on with Crissy and all her activities at her age. I'm becoming too much of a supermom. I hardly have time for myself and my yoga sessions."

Then Jen took off one Friday so that the family could take a long weekend at the cabin. On the way there, Bruce wanted to stop at the Hilltop to get sandwiches. Bruce's mother was in the car, as she was meeting Bruce's father at the cabin and they were going to go somewhere else for the weekend. Crissy wanted to stay in the car with Grandma, so Bruce and Jen went into the restaurant section to order, and there was Ben. Jen hadn't noticed his truck in the parking lot. Their eyes met, and they smiled, but nothing else transpired.

The next week when Ben came into the office the air was thick with his jealousy. Looking for reassurance that it was her husband, he asked, "Who was that guy I saw you with at the Hilltop?" With this confrontation Ben almost crossed a line in terms of safe conversation in the office, but Jen managed a snappy comeback: "Oh, you don't need to be jealous. It was only my husband." She maintained her composure, but her heart was racing.

After that, Ben's demeanor became more subdued whenever he came to the office. Jen sensed that he was hurt. She felt guilty, but she maintained her reserve around him, and eventually Ben matched her reserve, making seeing each other at the office easier.

Part of Jen was hurting for Ben, and part was relieved. The affair was finally over. She had sacrificed her fun, carefree side in order to end her obsession with Ben—even though he was still on her mind.

REDEFINING RESPONSIBILITY

As therapy continued, some questions were arising: Could freedom and responsibility coexist? Could Jen find that sense of freedom in her relationship with Bruce?

Before Crissy was born, Bruce seemed to relish his freedom, expressing it in a variety of "irresponsible" ways, as Jen put it, and yet it was at that very point in time that she wanted to rescue him. Now Jen had become the one who was the irresponsible one, by having an affair. This thought was foremost in her mind when she entered the next ecstatic trance experience using the Lady of Cholula, a divination posture. After the induction ritual and sitting in this posture for the fifteen minutes that I drummed, she related her trance experience:

"I went back to taking off Daddy's work boots and bringing him his slippers. He was very responsible in his work in construction. In looking back I wondered if he was unhappy coming home so tired, but then I remembered the times we were driving together around town and he was always very proud to point out the houses and buildings he had helped build. He was proud of and seemed to enjoy the hard work he did, and he enjoyed coming home and plopping down in his chair. Bruce is proud of his success in sales and also likes coming home and plopping down in his chair with Crissy beside him.

"I then thought of Mom and the way she would plop down in her chair after her day of housework, cooking, and caring for us. She always seemed to have more to do and would do it. I don't know if she felt proud, but when she would have family and friends over to visit, the house was spotless, so she may have taken pride in that. I'm not sure that freedom from responsibility had anything to do with their enjoyment of life. Pride seems more relevant. Yet their hard work gave them the freedom to enjoy friends and family. Bruce's hard work gives him the freedom to enjoy the hunting camp when he wants to, and even there he enjoys working on things. He has always helped around the house and often cooks since we both work. He seems to really enjoy his free time."

The Lady of Cholula experience took Jen deeper into thinking about responsibility and freedom. I asked her, "What does this experience say about you?"

"My job has responsibilities, but I can't say I take pride in what I do."

"You mentioned that when you leave the office there is another person who can handle the incoming invoices. Do you appreciate her doing this for you?"

"Oh, that's her job. That's just one of many office clerical tasks that we do. We are friends, and we enjoy our time together, but I don't think it's necessary to appreciate what she does or for her to appreciate what I do. It's just what we're supposed to do."

"At home do you take pride in what you do for Bruce and Crissy?"

"Bruce does as much as I do. We work together. It's just like it is at the office."

"Do you take pride in your home when others visit?"

"I guess so. That doesn't happen very often. We're so busy with work and caring for Crissy."

"You don't seem to take pride in what you do like your parents did, like Bruce does."

"I guess you're right. I may have taken pride in getting Bruce to be more responsible, but it was Bruce who decided to do that. I don't take any pride in having an affair, and that's a much bigger issue."

"It sounds like the issue is taking pride in responsibility, more than it is taking pride in finding freedom from not taking responsibility.

Next week let's take this into the underworld of your unconscious mind to see if there is a way for you to take pride in your responsibilities."

With that, at our next session we used the Jivaro posture to explore where we had left off with this idea. After our usual induction ritual, and following fifteen minutes of drumming, Jen related her experience:

"I went back to the scene of pulling off Daddy's boots and getting him his slippers. He smiled at me and ruffled my hair. I helped a lot around the house, but Mom never did show much appreciation. I'm not sure, but maybe part of me was trying to find that appreciation and approval, and Daddy showed a little. Bruce does a much better job in showing me his appreciation. Crissy seems to enjoy sitting with her daddy on the couch after work. He's proud of her, and she feels it. He enjoys sitting with me, but I'm often too busy. I need to show Crissy I'm proud of her. I think as I grew up, being 'humble' was important and being proud was thought of as a sin."

"What do you feel proud of?"

"I can't think of anything."

"It's important to be a good mother and show Crissy that you are proud of her, something that seemed to be hard for your mother to do with you."

After this session, Jen expressed that her life was such that she felt like she was ready for therapy to wind down. The affair was clearly over, and she was feeling much more fulfilled at home with Bruce and Crissy, feeling like she was ready to make that commitment without sacrificing her happiness. When she saw Ben at work, nothing inappropriate would be said or even felt. At times she thought of the affair, but she knew that thoughts cannot be erased. Even though everything was going well for her, Jen said she wanted to come back for another session in two weeks, after Bruce's birthday celebration, an event she was in the process of planning.

NAGGING THOUGHTS

When Jen returned for the session after Bruce's birthday party, she was upset over a dream she had had the night after the party: "I was in the office when Ben came in. He needed me to come out to the truck to check some invoice numbers. The numbers didn't match because the vendor had made a substitution, and the discrepancy would cause a computer problem when the barcodes were scanned. This problem was not unusual, but it had been some time since I had been alone with Ben. Ben was behind me as I bent over to scan the codes. I knew he was taking off his clothes, so when I turned around I wasn't surprised. He had an enormous erection. I was so turned on I got down and took it in my mouth. I woke up in a panic, soaking with sweat."

"Wow! Ben wanted or needed to have you come with him. You were ready for him, turned on, and you accepted his invitation. What do you make of it?"

Jen broke down. "It's so hard to let go of him. I thought I was doing okay, but the dream brought everything back. What am I going to do?" Jen's innocence, her confidence that everything was okay, seemed to have abandoned her. "What am I going to do?" she sobbed.

"The dream may tell you more."

"What more can it tell me, that I can't say no or I won't say no?"

"That you feel powerless because you have no control over your sexual feelings."

"Yes!"

"But you have shown control over the last few months. You've taken charge of your feelings and said no."

"But I still want him," she said angrily.

Even though nothing had happened between her and Ben for several months, Jen still was punishing herself for her sexual feelings toward him. That was what she needed to do at this time to avoid the danger of falling into complacency. It appeared that she needed to feel guilty, and her dream ignited that guilt. Her unconscious mind actually rescued her from her complacency, a rescue that needed to be supported in therapy.

"What am I going to do?" Again that question.

"You're still beating yourself up over your sexual feelings toward Ben. You're still missing something in life, someone who makes you feel free and alive. Your understanding of your dream was so quick. There are many levels to a dream. Let's do a little more dream work. Who or what is Ben in your dream? *You* created this dream in your unconscious mind. *You* created Ben, an image of Ben, an image that is not necessarily the real Ben. In your dream, Ben, a man, takes off his clothes, has an erection, and this turns you on, makes you feel free and alive. Let's continue to pursue what it is you need in life, something that will give you satisfaction. Let's use the Feathered Serpent posture to let those fearful feelings die." I hoped that these feelings could be replaced with the birth of healthy pride.

After fifteen minutes standing in the Feathered Serpent, Jen reported, "I know that what I need to do is to find something that I'm proud of. I have been telling Crissy how proud I am of her, and that feels good. I'm proud of how she is growing and of the daughter we are raising. She is physically active, and I think she would be good at doing something physical like dancing or gymnastics. I mentioned it to Bruce, and he thought it was a good idea too. One of her friends is taking gymnastics, and we thought she would enjoy doing this with her friend. The lessons are once a week after school. Since we both work, her friend's mother could take her, and then we could get there to pick her up before the lessons are over, though I wish we could be there for the whole lesson. It seems like all the kids have so many other extracurricular lessons. When I was a kid hardly anyone took lessons except maybe piano or some musical instrument."

"Just imagine yourself going to a gymnastics meet. Can you feel the pride you would have in watching Crissy perform?"

"Uh-huh! That is just what I was thinking."

"That sounds like a good beginning, becoming more involved in Crissy's life and in parenting. Work schedules these days often make that somewhat difficult."

"That would also make it more difficult to find time to think about Ben," she added.

Ben was still on her mind, but as things developed over the next couple of weeks, Ben was not the only "extracurricular" Jen thought about. She came into therapy one day and told me, "I've been having a lot of thoughts about . . . about another man, Barry, a man who bought a cabin about a half mile down the road from us. We met last week. Bruce and Crissy were out for a walk, and he came by while they were gone and introduced himself. I was sitting out sunning myself. We only talked for a few minutes."

I replied, "If it weren't Ben, then it might be someone else who would fill your need of being free and alive, right? Bruce and Crissy don't do it. They're responsibilities. Maybe there is more? Go back to . . . what was his name, Barry? Another *B*. You seem to have some sort of attraction to *B*s. Stay with your feelings of when you met Barry. Tell me more about them."

"We were alone in front of the cabin. I was lounging in my bikini. This good-looking man walks up, and we smile at each other. I felt a rush when he smiled, quickly turned my hand to hide my ring. He told me who he was, and I told him my name. I didn't mention Bruce or Crissy, though that was stupid. Crissy's toys were scattered around, and I'm sure there was Bruce's stuff too."

"You wanted him to think of you as single. Think for a few moments about the stages of a woman's life: the virgin-maiden, the lover, the mother, and the crone. Feel the energy of the young girl, the carefree feeling of your childhood. But then you grow into a young woman and begin to feel sexual energy flowing through you. That feeling is exciting, but carried with it is the fear that you could become pregnant. Then when you do become pregnant, you are on the road to being responsible for a child. Think of the transitions that take place on this journey of becoming a mother, of losing the freedom and carefreeness of being the child. Being the lover is exciting, and in these times being the lover does not need to be frightening because of birth control. What's a healthy transition through these stages, and what interferes with these transitions? Where are you emotionally on this journey? You're a good mother, but you also seek the freedom of being the lover and feel hampered by the responsibility of being a mother. What's going on? Step back and picture yourself moving through these stages of life. What do you see? Not a quick answer, but something to contemplate with patience, gentleness, and curiosity. This is a good place to end the session, with something to think about during this next week."

THE LOST CHILDHOOD

A new issue had been raised in Jen's therapy, that of maturity, of getting older, and the fears of aging. This suggested that we take this to the Lady of Cholula. Maybe there was something else that prevented Jen from accepting the responsibility of marriage and parenthood. The something else might be the reason she was not ready to be the responsible wife and mother. I suggested, "Let's take another look at what responsibility means to you."

After the induction ritual and as the drumming started, I suggested, "Take the word *responsible* to the Lady of Cholula. Remember when you sold Strawberry because she was too much responsibility and you wanted to have the time to spend with your friends? Take that feeling of responsibility back even further in time."

As she went into trance, Jen almost immediately started to speak. "My mom and dad were always talking about responsibility. Whenever I started something, and if I even mentioned not wanting to continue, they would bring up that it was not responsible to stop, whether it was junior high softball or taking piano lessons. I hated that word. I remember telling myself I would never use that word with my children. In the sixth grade I had a paper to write. The teacher gave us a choice of topics. I started on one topic and then changed my mind. Mom had a fit, even when I explained to her I had plenty of time and the other topic sounded more interesting. She told me I was irresponsible to be wasting time. I hated that word *responsibility.*"

The drumming continued. I prompted, "Have your adult self go back and be with your younger self, and with all the wisdom and understanding of your adult self, help your younger self better understand."

"Kids need to be free of responsibility. Responsibility is for grown-ups. I was never free as a kid. I always had to be responsible. I was cheated."

"You've been cheated. You don't want to be a responsible adult. You want to feel the freedom of what it means to be a kid."

Jen was able to weep for the child she never could be, but she couldn't weep for being the irresponsible adult. She was still carrying with her the pain of being cheated, and she was cheating her husband and daughter because of it. Yet she was now ready to face this issue of hating responsibility. She was an adult and knew about the responsibilities of adulthood, of being a wife and a mother. She was learning to appreciate the pride she could take in being a mother and was preparing herself to shake off the stigma of what that word *responsibility* meant to her. In her affair with Ben she had been thumbing her nose at responsibility, attempting to experience the carefree feeling of an affair without responsibility, but never attaining a truly carefree feeling because her feelings of guilt interfered. She had finally been successful in breaking off with Ben, but there was still this issue of hating responsibility, and the appearance of another *B* man, Barry, was now forcing her to once again face the crux of the situation.

Jen's escape from responsibility was quite evident in the following dream she related in this session: "I was changing Crissy's dirty diaper. It was crazy—Crissy has been out of diapers for over a year, and I really had no problems with changing her diapers before. But I was saying to myself, *Why do I have to do this? Crissy is old enough to not dirty her diaper.* I was feeling very resentful. I know kids sometimes have accidents, but I was expecting Crissy to be an adult and take care of herself. I called to Bruce to come and finish the job, and I walked away smiling to myself, feeling free, but still I knew I should have done it."

Jen's use of the words *resentful* and *free* made it quite apparent to me that she already understood the dream's meaning, at least unconsciously. The only important word she left out was *responsibility*. I asked her anyway what she made of this dream. "It's the same old struggle—having to be responsible and resenting my lack of freedom."

There, she used the word. "It couldn't be clearer," I said. "Even though you have ended the affair, at least outwardly, the struggle is still alive inside you."

PLAYING WITH FIRE

The next week Jen told me about another dream she'd had:

"I was at the cabin by myself, doing some project there, and I felt so free. I don't remember the project, but I think I had the sewing machine set up on the front porch. Anyway, I was wearing my bikini. Crissy was running around naked, squealing after her bath, feeling so free out of her diapers. Feeling free myself, I took off my top while I was sewing.

"This dream got me to thinking that I never go to the cabin by myself, and I should—I could make curtains for the cabin windows. I have no idea whether Barry would be there or not. Bruce happened to tell his father about what I was thinking about doing, and he called to tell me that the windows have never had curtains all these years; why would I want to put them up now and have to take them down to wash later? To him it seemed like an unnecessary project. But Bruce thought it would be good for me to get away by myself and told me not to worry about what his father said. I just wanted to run around free in my bikini or even less. So I went up last weekend to make curtains. Barry did show up, but nothing happened. He just had a question about the area, where to take his trash. I didn't see him after that. I felt mixed up—both relieved and disappointed. I could have been sitting at the sewing machine topless. I probably would have freaked. I did take my top off after he left. Why shouldn't I feel that freedom when out in the woods? Guys do it all the time."

I responded, "Nothing happened, and you felt both disappointed and relieved. It also sounds like you are trying to justify why it's okay to sit on the porch topless, maybe hoping that Barry might find some reason to come back? Your feelings were mixed up. Thinking about Barry is exciting, but you would be right back into feeling guilty, and it would demolish your integrity. You just can't be responsible and feel free at the same time."

At this moment Jen was very much in touch with her feelings and was able to quickly put the thoughts of her unconscious mind into words. It was the perfect time to use the Lady of Cholula posture.

"There is something else going on within you," I said. "Let's try to find out by asking the Lady of Cholula. You so much resent responsibility, yet you are a very responsible person. Even in school the decisions you made that your parents called irresponsible turned out to be quite responsible. I am thinking that all healthy adolescents need to rebel, to make their own decisions at some point. Sometimes they're healthy ones and sometimes not, but they need to undertake that exploration at some point."

After going through the induction ritual and the fifteen minutes of drumming sitting in the Lady of Cholula posture, Jen related the following:

"One of my friends got pregnant. She was quite promiscuous. I guess my rebellion was being, in my parents' words, *irresponsible*. My parents thought it was irresponsible to marry Bruce, who at the time had no direction in life. That may have been their greatest disappointment. But when Bruce got his act together, they were happy."

"Your rebellion lost its power when he became responsible."

"But who am I rebelling against, my parents or Bruce?"

"You were happy when Bruce became responsible, and you yourself have always been responsible, as much as you resent that word, except when you married Bruce. You have so much insight into people; probably you sensed that part of Bruce that was responsible but found his irresponsibility to be carefree and exciting."

In the succeeding weeks, Jen made a couple of trips to the family's hunting cabin to enjoy a sense of being carefree and on her own. Going there and sitting on the front porch with her sewing machine to make curtains felt like freedom. Being away from her husband and daughter, sitting on the porch in the woods topless in the sun, really invigorated her. What could be more innocent than her back-to-nature experience?

On one of these trips she went by Barry's cabin just to see what it was like. If he had been there she would have simply considered it a welcome-to-the-neighborhood kind of visit. He wasn't, however. It was a nice cabin in a beautiful location situated near the creek, with a deck that extended out to the edge of the water. She told me she fantasized about lounging on the deck with Barry. Later, when she got home, she noticed a sale of redwood yard furniture at a local store and immediately thought of Barry's deck. She found time to go by the sale and bought a redwood lounge chair. It was a good price, she explained to Bruce. She told her husband it would be a nice housewarming, or cabinwarming, gift for Barry, "our new neighbor." Bruce thought the gift was extravagant but only said, "Whatever . . ."

When Jen mentioned to Bruce a week later that she was going back to the cabin, he observed, "You're going up there a lot these days, but whatever."

"I want to finish the curtains, and I have been enjoying the time by myself, three or four hours on a Saturday afternoon. It gives you some time alone with Crissy, and that is very special to Crissy to be alone with her dad." So Jen went up to the cabin that Saturday and on her way dropped the lounge chair off on Barry's deck with a note, signing it from Jen, Bruce, and Crissy.

The next time the whole family went up, they saw Barry. The first thing Barry said was that he could not accept the chair. Bruce was embarrassed, but Jen said, "Oh, it's nothing, sure you can."

Barry answered, "Well, okay, thank you, it's really nice," and Jen gave him a quick hug.

I asked Jen about what she was imagining, first when leaving the lounge chair on Barry's deck and then when she gave him the hug.

She looked a little guilty, and her answer was slow in coming. It was obvious her imagination was in overdrive. "Oh, nothing. I just thought it would be nice to give him a housewarming gift. There aren't many people up there to welcome anybody, and it's nice to get to know your neighbors for security and all, someone to keep an eye on your cabin. We've had our cabin broken into a couple of times . . . He seems to be there alone. If something happens, it's good to have someone to call . . . We exchanged cell phone numbers for emergencies. Who knows what would happen if I was up there alone? We've seen bears several times. If I was up there alone and saw a bear, I'd have Barry's number to call."

I smiled, "Wishful thinking."

Jen sheepishly nodded in the affirmative.

"Isn't Bruce worried about the bears when you go up alone?"

"Oh, no! He knows I don't wander far from the cabin or the car. We've talked a lot about the bears to Crissy, that they can be dangerous and she needs to stay close to the cabin and run inside if she sees one."

"From what you said, isn't Bruce becoming a little suspicious?"

"I don't think so. Maybe a little resentful that I like to get away and leave Crissy with him. I don't think he thinks anything about Barry."

"But you do. Barry doesn't know that you're not afraid of bears. If you called him, by the time he got there the bear would be long gone."

Again Jen looked sheepish. "Oh, nothing's going to happen. We're rarely there at the same time anyway."

With that, we took an ecstatic journey with the Jivaro posture to journey into her unconscious mind to examine more deeply her need to rebel and whom she was rebelling against.

At the conclusion of the session, Jen commented, "The question was quickly and directly answered. You mentioned the last time that when Bruce became responsible, my rebellion lost its power. I guess I am somewhat rebelling against Bruce because he took that power of rebelling against my parents away by becoming respectable in their eyes. But that sounds pretty immature . . ." Jen was clearly gaining insights into her own unconscious drives.

Several weeks later, Jen came to therapy in a very different mood—much more subdued. She and her family had gone to the cabin, and Barry had come over for a visit, it turned out, to introduce his wife. "She was very attractive. I could see that Barry was really in love with her." Jen's balloon had been popped. After this brief interlude with irresponsibility she was again ready to work on what responsibility and freedom meant to her.

THE IMPORTANCE OF SECURITY

My sessions with Jen were down to about two a month for the last couple of months since Jen had decidedly ended her affair with Ben. Between our last two sessions she had made a trip with Crissy to see her mother in Florida. On previous trips they almost always stayed in the same motel on the way there, and while she was there she had this dream:

"In the dream, when we got to the motel I moved our stuff from our suitcases into the dresser like I do in real life, but in the dream there was no dresser in the room, only a couple of stools for holding the suitcases. I laid the suitcases out, and we got ready for bed, but I felt real agitated. That was the dream. Not much to it. So what if there was no dresser? We were only going to be there overnight. Bruce always thinks it makes no sense to move stuff into a motel dresser, but I always like to. He just opens his suitcase on the floor. It makes me feel more at home to use the dresser. That's why motel rooms have dressers anyway."

"So let's take the dream of the motel with no dresser to a different level with the Feathered Serpent." After the induction ritual and standing in the posture for several minutes, she interrupted the drumming to tell me the following:

"I feel more secure in my own space. I felt that with the cabin. After I made the curtains I overheard Bruce and his dad having a disagreement. His dad was not at all happy about the curtains and complained that it didn't feel like his cabin anymore. Bruce defended me, telling him that it was my cabin too, and that it made me happy to decorate it with curtains. It was no big deal to Bruce, especially since he didn't have to wash the curtains. Making it more my space makes me feel more secure, especially when we are traveling. Bruce says that he feels more free when traveling to leave most of the stuff in the car; that way it's easier to pick up and leave in the morning."

"But you feel more free when you feel more secure, in this case by making a space your own."

"Yeah."

"But there is more responsibility in making your own space, whether it is unpacking and repacking or washing the curtains."

"Yeah, I guess so."

"You didn't tell me you were going to Florida. Was that a spur-of-the-moment decision?"

"Uh-huh. Mom suggested we come down for a visit, and I thought it would be nice. School has started, so everyone else at work was back from their vacations, and I had more vacation time I needed to use up, so we left Bruce at home and took off for six days. Crissy always likes to see Grandma, and Mom misses her granddaughter. Plus next year Crissy will be in school, so it won't be as easy to get away."

"That must have felt free, impulsive, to so easily get away from all of your responsibilities. Your mother didn't think that was being irresponsible to just pick up and take off like that?"

"Oh no! She hadn't seen us since Christmas. She probably thought that was the responsible thing to do."

"So, back to your dream. You feel free when you're on the road and take the responsibility of making a space your own, and you feel insecure and agitated when you don't have that opportunity."

"That's a problem when visiting Mom. She lives in a one-bedroom apartment. When Bruce goes, we always stay in a motel, but with just the two of us we stayed on her hide-a-bed and didn't have a dresser of our own. Three nights there was a long time."

"Whenever you got together with Ben I bet you never had a space to make your own."

"That's what's nice about being married to Bruce. We own our home, and I feel secure in making it my space. It's really my space. I wouldn't want to lose that. That's another reason I was agitated about the affair."

"But a home is a big responsibility. Take a moment to listen to the agitation, the insecurity in your dream. Where else in your life do you feel such agitation and insecurity?"

The drumming continued as we talked. "In the cabin curtains and the Barry dream, my mixed-up feelings could be described the same way, agitated."

"This motel dresser dream helps give you a better name for your mixed-up feelings in the cabin curtain and Barry dream. Thinking of Barry causes you to feel agitated and insecure. Stay with those feelings and thoughts for a few moments. Feelings that are experienced in dreams are very deep feelings. Let those feelings help you appreciate the security of your home."

I sensed that contentment was growing in Jen. The word *responsibility* had a different connotation in the context of the security of her own home. She couldn't let the carefree excitement of having an affair destroy what she so valued. Jen was beginning to find a sense of security in the balance between freedom and responsibility.

Jen's struggle to accept her role as a responsible adult had been the catalyst to take her to a new level of self-awareness. She learned to accept responsibility not as a burden, but as something that defined her and provided her with a sense of security as a mother and wife. She found that freedom and self-respect could coexist, and she no longer needed to pursue excitement in the form of extramarital affairs. With her new understanding about what responsibility really meant, she had found the strength to give up her need to act out an immature drive to rebel.

Jen moved beyond her self-centered need to rebel and be irresponsible. She was now truly part of her family in a healthy and mature way. Her deeper insights into her feelings and behaviors were a central strength to bring her to this level of consciousness. Both her practice of yoga and the ritual to induce ecstatic trance helped her into new life situations that showed her the value of a wide range of cultural diversity and spirituality.

As I do with all clients with whom I use ecstatic trance postures, at the conclusion of our therapy I told Jen about my ecstatic trance group, which is free of charge, and she expressed interest in continuing her journey on the path of conscious evolution. Her enthusiasm would be a benefit to the group, and I could see her maturing to become a leader in this work.

Epilogue

Coyote . . . teaching us how silly we look to the gods when we take ourselves too seriously.

LEWIS MEHL-MADRONA

Thomas Berry says that to save the Earth and ourselves from destruction we humans need to rediscover what the hunter-gatherer cultures have long known—that we are no better than any of the flora and fauna of the Earth; we are rather *interdependent* with all life forms and substances of the Earth.[1] We are not the culmination of evolution, but one small step in the process of evolution. We experience this interdependency in our dreams and in our waking visions, both of which are trance states. Doing so, we regain the shamanic capabilities that all human beings are endowed with.

The shaman is a healer. The people bring their ailments, whether physical, emotional, or interpersonal, to the shaman. He or she is thus a combination physician, psychologist, and social worker. To accomplish the task of healing, the shaman calls on the source energy to which we are connected: the ancestors, who have taught and continue to teach the people (at least the people who were and are part of hunter-gatherer societies); the Earth spirits and Mother Earth herself, who sustains all life; and the universal mind, that vast field of knowledge beyond our individual sensory perceptions, which gives us access to the knowledge of what is happening at a distance, what has happened in the past, and what can be expected in the future—knowledge that is time-free and transparent.

These healing forces are brought to bear on the confusion that arises from the mental state of dualistic thinking, allowing us to integrate the disparate parts of ourselves to attain wholeness and transformation. This is the true freedom of the human being. It is a process of growing and becoming, but most of all it is a *process,* a lifelong journey that can take us all the way to self-mastery. This is the meaning and purpose underlying the ecstatic trance postures as discovered and elucidated by Felicitas Goodman.

Shamans are traditionally thought of as special people who have special powers. But we now know that anyone can learn the powers of the shaman, as evidenced in the previous case studies and the numerous personal experiences I have had and have witnessed others having over the many years I have worked with the ecstatic trance postures, as detailed in my previous books: *The Power of Ecstatic Trance, Baldr's Magic,* and *Beowulf's Ecstatic Trance Magic.* These books, along with the one you now hold in your hands, describe the process and procedures that can be used for healing on the personal, communal, and ultimately the planetary level.

The lives of hunter-gatherer peoples were (and are, for the few such peoples who still inhabit the Earth) directed by rituals that guide people into altered states of reality for healing purposes. These rituals were learned by parents, who learned them from their parents, who learned them from their parents, all the way back through the ancestors, with the ancestors being the first to provide the rituals of living that guide the life of the community and keep everything in balance. The shaman expresses gratitude to the ancestors and calls on them, reminding us of our connection to the rituals of life that the ancestors discovered brought greater harmony, both personally and communally. We do this in our ecstatic trance posture work.

We now know that our very survival in these precarious times depends on humanity's recognition that everything of the Earth is interdependent, and this interdependency is what sustains life. For this reason the shaman calls on animal spirit guides and spirit guides in other forms and substances of the Earth, in order to integrate with the Earth. In traditional cultures there are dances and rituals that involve calling on the spirit guides while costumed in the garb of the spirit guides, as the enactors, in trance, shape-shift to become the spirit guide. In this way shamanic cultures experience everything of the Earth as an ancestor. We do the same kind of calling of the spirits and shape-shifting in our ecstatic trance posture work.

Finally, we connect to source energy when as our shamanic selves we commune with the universal mind. This connection takes us to other timelines and other dimensions for the healing of collective and planetary karma—the aim of all those spiritual explorers who endeavor to evolve beyond the limited, personal, self-centered consciousness that has resulted in so much pain and suffering on our planet, and who are committed to the spiritual maturation of humanity. It's a fascinating journey that I experienced almost from the start in working with the ecstatic trance postures; again, it is the subject of my previous books.

Psychologists and physicians concern themselves with diagnosing and treating the problems of the individual. Insurance companies pay for this treatment depending on the individual's diagnosis. Treatment of problems of the family, community, and society is not considered relevant. The power of ecstatic trance takes healing beyond the limited scope of conventional psychotherapy and its dualistic conventional medical model. The shaman—who is the ecstatic trance journeyer—seeks to bring harmony to the wider world of the family, the community, society, all of humanity, and all that is of our great Earth Mother.

Appendix
About Ecstatic Trance

There is a growing body of work available on ecstatic trance, beginning with Felicitas Goodman's foundational book *Where the Spirits Ride the Wind: Trance Journeys and Other Ecstatic Experiences*. A student of hers, Belinda Gore, who has been my mentor in my work with ecstatic trance, has published two books that catalog the ecstatic postures: *Ecstatic Body Postures: An Alternate Reality Workbook* and *The Ecstatic Experience: Healing Postures for Spirit Journeys*. In addition to these three books, Felicitas Goodman and Nana Nauwald wrote *Ecstatic Trance: New Ritual Body Postures,* originally published in German and now available in English. Another German resource is Annette Ki Salmen's *Mohnfrau: Wege zur heilung durch trance*. Salmen taught me the way of soul retrieval using the ecstatic postures at a workshop at the Cuyamungue Institute in New Mexico (many papers written about ecstatic trance are available on the institute's website, www.cuyamungueinstitute.com).

I have written four books on ecstatic trance. The first was *The Power of Ecstatic Trance: Practices for Healing, Spiritual Growth, and Accessing the Universal Mind*. This book provides many examples of the power of ecstatic trance, including incidents of healing, time regression to ancient ancestral times, and reading the mind of another person (as so frequently when in an altered trance state I find myself experiencing the experience of another person who is in my presence). The next two books, *Baldr's Magic: The Power of Norse Shamanism and Ecstatic Trance,* and *Beowulf's Ecstatic Trance Magic: Accessing the Archaic*

Powers of the Universal Mind, deal with my experiences going back to ancient times to commune with my own ancestors and ancestors of the land. For the hunter-gatherers, communing with their ancestors was central to their way of relating to the world and learning how to live. My fourth book is *Trance Journeys of the Hunter-Gatherers: Ecstatic Practices to Reconnect with the Great Mother and Heal the Earth.* For the hunter-gatherer peoples, their experience of the Earth and nature was quite different from ours. They felt at one with the Earth and lived in harmony with everything of the Earth without feeling superior to any other life-form. This book provides many examples of how ecstatic trance returns us to this experience of oneness with the Earth and shows us that we are just one small step in the process of evolution.

The role of the hunter-gatherer shaman includes healing or restoring harmony within the individual and the community; communing with ancestors, the teachers of the community's way of life; understanding and attaining oneness with all life and everything of the Earth; and going beyond in accessing information from the trans-sensory universal mind. Each of my books has used ecstatic trance to accomplish these shamanic activities. Though for the shaman many other activities are important, this book, *Ecstatic Soul Retrieval: Shamanism and Psychotherapy,* is intended to take the healing role of the shaman to a deeper level in restoring harmony. To restore harmony is to restore a lost part of oneself, one's original innocence. Retrieving this innocence is to retrieve the soul.

Notes

I. INTRODUCTION TO ECSTATIC TRANCE IN THE THERAPEUTIC SETTING

1. Baudouin, *Suggestion,* 116.
2. Araoz, *New Hypnosis,* 4.
3. Watkins, "Affect bridge."
4. Brink, "Age Regression."
5. Barnett, *Analytical Hypnotherapy,* 108–16.
6. Erickson, Rossi, and Rossi, *Hypnotic Realities,* 58.
7. Goodman, *Where the Spirits,* 16.
8. Ibid., 16.
9. Ibid., 18–26.
10. Emerson, "Can Belief Systems Influence Neurophysiology?"
11. Laszlo and Combs, *Thomas Berry, Dreamer of the Earth,* 6, 20.

2. ADAPTING ECSTATIC TRANCE TO PSYCHOTHERAPY

1. Brink, "Age Regression"; and Watkins, "Affect bridge," 21–27.
2. Barrett, "Royal"; Gonçalves and João, "From Reactive"; Leijssen, "Focusing"; and Hill and Rochlen, "Hill Cognitive-Experiential."
3. Beck, *Cognitive Therapy and the Emotional Disorders,* 36.
4. Brink, "Age Regression."
5. Rosner, "Aaron T. Beck's Dream Theory in Context."
6. Erickson, Rossi, and Rossi, *Hypnotic Realities,* 58.

7. Personal website of David Korten, http://livingeconomiesforum.org /author-bio.

8. Korten, *Great Turning,* 43–44.

9. Ibid., 44–46

10. Ibid., 46–47.

11. Ray and Anderson, *Cultural Creatives,* 7–42.

12. Ibid., front matter.

13. Barnett, *Analytic Hypnotherapy,* 120–24.

4. TRANSFORMING ANGER
TO TRANSFORM RELATIONSHIPS

1. Chenille Sisters, "I Lie."

5. BALANCING FREEDOM AND RESPONSIBILITY

1. Yapko, *Treating Depression with Hypnosis.*

EPILOGUE

1. Combs, "University," 6.

Bibliography

Araoz, Daniel L. *The New Hypnosis: Techniques in Brief Individual and Family Psychotherapy.* New York: Brunner/Mazel, 1985.

Barnett, Edgar. *Analytical Hypnotherapy: Principles and Practices.* London: Westwood, 1981.

Barrett, Deirdre. "The 'Royal Road' Becomes a Shrewd Shortcut: The Use of Dreams in Focused Treatment." In *Cognitive Therapy and Dreams,* edited by Rachael Rosner, William Lyddon, and Arthur Freeman, 113–24. New York: Springer, 2004.

Baudouin, Charles. *Suggestion and Auto-Suggestion.* London: George Allen and Unwin Ltd., 1979.

Beck, Aaron T. *Cognitive Therapy and the Emotional Disorders.* New York: Meridian/Penguin, 1978.

Braden, Gregg. *The Divine Matrix: Bridging Time, Space, Miracles, and Beliefs.* Carlsbad, Calif.: Hay House. 2007.

Brink, Nicholas E. "Age Regression." *Corsini Encyclopedia of Psychology, Vol. 1, A-C.* Edited by Irving Weiner and Edward Craighead. Hoboken, N.J.: John Wiley and Sons, 2010.

———. *Baldr's Magic: The Power of Norse Shamanism and Ecstatic Trance.* Rochester, Vt.: Bear & Company, 2014.

———. *Beowulf's Ecstatic Trance Magic: Accessing the Archaic Powers of the Universal Mind.* Rochester, Vt.: Bear & Company, 2016.

———. *Grendel and His Mother: Healing the Traumas of Childhood through Dreams, Imagery and Hypnosis.* Amityville, N.Y.: Baywood, 2002.

———. *The Power of Ecstatic Trance: Practices for Healing, Spiritual Growth, and Accessing the Universal Mind.* Rochester, Vt.: Bear & Company, 2013.

———. *Trance Journeys of the Hunter-Gatherers: Ecstatic Practices to Reconnect with the Great Mother and Heal the Earth.* Rochester, Vt.: Bear & Company, 2016.

Chenille Sisters. "I Lie in the Dark." *Haute Chenille: A Retrospective.* St. Paul, Minn.: Red House Records, 1995.

Combs, Allan. "The University of the Earth: An Introduction to Thomas Berry." In *Thomas Berry, Dreamer of the Earth: The Spiritual Ecology of the Father of Environmentalism,* edited by Ervin Laszlo and Allan Combs, 1–8. Rochester, Vt.: Inner Traditions, 2011.

Emerson, V. F. "Can Belief Systems Influence Neurophysiology? Some Implications of Research on Meditation." *Newsletter-Review, R. M. Bucke Memorial Society* 5: 20–32.

Erickson, Milton, Ernest Rossi, and Sheila Rossi. *Hypnotic Realities: The Induction of Clinical Hypnosis and Forms of Indirect Suggestion.* New York: Irvington Publishers, 1977.

Gonçalves, Óscar, and Barbara João. "From Reactive to Proactive Dreaming," 125–36, in *Cognitive Therapy and Dreams.* Edited by Rachael Rosner, William Lyddon, and Arthur Freeman. New York: Springer, 2004.

Goodman, Felicitas. *Where the Spirits Ride the Wind: Trance Journeys and Other Ecstatic Experiences.* Bloomington: Indiana University Press, 1990.

Goodman, Felicitas, and Nana Nauwald. *Ecstatic Trance: New Ritual Body Postures, a Workbook.* Havelte, Holland: Binkey Kok Publications, 2003.

Gore, Belinda. *Ecstatic Body Postures: An Alternate Reality Workbook.* Rochester, Vt.: Bear & Company, 1995.

———. *The Ecstatic Experience: Healing Postures for Spirit Journeys.* Rochester, Vt.: Bear & Company, 2009.

Hill, Clara E., ed. *Dream Work in Therapy: Facilitating Exploration, Insight and Action.* Washington, D.C.: American Psychological Association Press, 2004.

Hill, Clara E., and Aaron Rochlen. "The Hill Cognitive-Experiential Model of Dream Interpretation." In *Cognitive Therapy and Dreams,* edited by Rachael Rosner, William Lyddon, and Arthur Freeman, 161–80. New York: Springer, 2004.

Jung, Carl. *The Portable Jung.* Edited by Joseph Campbell, translated by R. F. C. Hull. New York: Penguin, 1976.

Korten, David. *The Great Turning: From Empire to Earth Community.* San Francisco: Berrett-Koehler Publishing, 2006.

Krippner, Stanley, Michael Bova, and Leslie Gray, eds. *Healing Stories: The Use of Narrative in Counseling and Psychotherapy.* Charlottesville, Va.: Puente Publications, 2007.

Kroger, William S. *Clinical and Experimental Hypnosis.* Philadelphia: Lippincott, 1963.

Laszlo, Ervin. *The Akashic Experience: Science and the Cosmic Memory Field.* Rochester, Vt.: Inner Traditions, 2009.

Laszlo, Ervin, and Alan Combs. *Thomas Berry, Dreamer of the Earth: The Spiritual Ecology of the Father of Environmentalism.* Rochester, Vt.: Inner Traditions, 2011.

Leijssen, Mia. "Focusing Oriented Dream Work," In *Cognitive Therapy and Dreams,* edited by Rachael Rosner, William Lyddon, and Arthur Freeman, 137–60. New York: Springer, 2004.

Mehl-Madrona, Lewis. *Healing the Mind Through the Power of Story: The Promise of Narrative Psychiatry.* Rochester, Vt.: Bear & Company, 2010.

Ray, Paul, and Sherry Ruth Anderson. *The Cultural Creatives: How 50 Million People Are Changing the World.* New York: Three Rivers Press, 2000.

Raynor, E. "Infinite experiences, affects and the characteristics of the unconscious." *International Journal of Psycho-analysis* 62 (1981): 403–12.

Rosner, Rachael. "Aaron T. Beck's Dream Theory in Context: An Introduction to His 1971 Article on Cognitive Patterns in Dreams and Daydreams." In *Cognitive Therapy and Dreams,* edited by Rachael Rosner, William Lyddon, and Arthur Freeman, 9–26. New York: Springer, 2004.

Salmen, Annette Ki. *Mohnfrau: Wege zur heilung durch trance.* Uhlstädt-Kirchhasel, Germany: Arun-Verlag, 2010.

Sarbin, Theodore, ed. *Narrative Psychology: The Storied Nature of Human Conduct.* Westport, Conn.: Praeger, 1986.

Sheldrake, Rupert. *A New Science of Life: The Hypothesis of Morphic Resonance.* Rochester, Vt.: Park Street Press, 1995.

Storm, Hyemeyohsts. *Seven Arrows.* New York: Harper and Row, 1972.

Watkins, John. "The affect bridge: A hypnoanalytic technique." *International Journal of Clinical and Experimental Hypnosis* 19 (1971): 21–27.

Yapko, Michael D. *Treating Depression with Hypnosis: Integrating Cognitive-Behavioral and Strategic Approaches.* Philadelphia: Routledge, 2001.

Index

Numbers in *italics* indicate illustrations.

BOOKS OF RELATED INTEREST

Trance Journeys of the Hunter-Gatherers
Ecstatic Practices to Reconnect with the Great Mother and Heal the Earth
by Nicholas E. Brink, Ph.D.

Beowulf's Ecstatic Trance Magic
Accessing the Archaic Powers of the Universal Mind
by Nicholas E. Brink, Ph.D.

Baldr's Magic
The Power of Norse Shamanism and Ecstatic Trance
by Nicholas E. Brink, Ph.D.

The Power of Ecstatic Trance
Practices for Healing, Spiritual Growth, and Accessing the Universal Mind
by Nicholas E. Brink, Ph.D.

Advanced Autogenic Training and Primal Awareness
Techniques for Wellness, Deeper Connection to Nature,
and Higher Consciousness
by James Endredy

The Ecstatic Experience
Healing Postures for Spirit Journeys
by Belinda Gore

Shapeshifting
Techniques for Global and Personal Transformation
by John Perkins

Speaking with Nature
Awakening to the Deep Wisdom of the Earth
by Sandra Ingerman and Llyn Roberts

INNER TRADITIONS • BEAR & COMPANY
P.O. Box 388
Rochester, VT 05767
1-800-246-8648
www.InnerTraditions.com

Or contact your local bookseller